# FE
# NC
# ED

*Fence* Volume 20, No. 1 Winterspring 2019
©2019 Fence Magazine, Incorporated

*Front Cover*: © Christopher Wool
Untitled, 1989
Enamel and acrylic on aluminum
72 x 48 inches
(182.88 x 121.92 cm)

*Back Cover*: © Christopher Wool
Untitled, 1989-90
Enamel on aluminum
96 x 60 inches
(243.8 x 152.4 cm)

*Fence* is published 2x/yr.

*Fence* receives submissions electronically at fence.submittable.com. Response time is between
three and nine months. Repeat publications take place after at least four issues or two years have
elapsed.

Find us at fenceportal.org or fence.fencebooks@gmail.com.
Or, at  (518) 567-7006.

This issue of *Fence* was printed in the United States by Versa Press. *Fence* is distributed in
North America by: Small Press Distribution, Berkeley, CA (510) 524-1668; and whatever giant
conglomerate has most recently swallowed TNG.

ISBN: 978-1-944380-15-1
ISSN: 1097-9980

*Fence*  is published by Fence Magazine, Incorporated, a not-for-profit corporation. Donations and
gifts are tax-deductible to the extent allowed by law.

*Fence* is made possible by the agency of the Fence Trust and all Friends of Fence. This project is
supported by awards from the Whiting Foundation, the National Endowment for the Arts, and the
New York State Council on the Arts.

A one-year subscription is $22; two-year subscription is $32. Membership is available at
fenceportal.org and offers a host of promises, if not privileges, including subscription and books
and entry and access.

If you'd like to support *Fence*, you can donate on our website, or contact Rebecca Wolff at
rebeccafence@gmail.com.

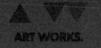

# Fence
## *35 winterspring 2019*

**FENCEPORTAL.ORG**

# FENCE

# NEW FROM FENCE BOOKS

## *LITE YEAR*

## TESS BROWN-LAVOIE

*A classical frame—the agricultural year, its gleanings and turnings—rendered in prismatic interiority with systemic digital criticality.*

"In Lite Year, Tess Brown-Lavoie flexes all the intricacies and ironies of the prose-poem form to navigate the absurd task of trying to live tenderly. Armed with vibrant syntax and an infectious sense of humor, these poems approach desire, power, illness, and "fragility et cetera" with a truly inventive voice. Epiphanies take place within a richly-textured urban pastoral—in Walgreens parking lots, in psychiatric hospitals, in front seats of sedans—as she draws maps for the largest and smallest of dooms. Throughout, Brown-Lavoie maintains the staggering intimacy of the letter to the beloved, or the letter to the self; to be called into such closeness is a gift."
FRANNY CHOI

"TESS BROWN-LAVOIE navigates the absurd and cosmic cycles of violence and self-care. Diseases flare. People relapse. Families coalesce and rupture. Plants break the surface of the earth. Time passes and language is just one method of notation as the body and the land register it all."
CAROLYN LAZARD, disability activist, writer

"BROWN-LAVOIE reminds us that— like fruit— we are ripest and sweetest when our skin is not as hard as it once was, but still finds a way to protect the bruises and softness of our meat." VICTORIA RUIZ, police abolitionist

"Unreadable my ass."
LAURA BROWN-LAVOIE

**WINNER OF THE FENCE MODERN POETS SERIES**

# SKINS OF COLUMBUS
## A DREAM ETHNOGRAPHY

### EDGAR GARCIA

*Colonial violence is a sticky phenomenon, gumming up the associational matrices of our daily lives and dreamscapes. Edgar Garcia intervenes with a poetic experiment: Every night of the three months of Columbus's first voyage to the Americas, Garcia read his corresponding journal entry before sleep. Asleep, his mind sutures displacements, migrations, and restorations into an assemblage of hemispheric becoming.*

Edgar Garcia is part of an exciting new cohort of Greater American poets who are working towards decoding & re-coding multi-metrical conceptions of historical space-time with the intent of reinvigorating political agencies. *Skins of Columbus* is a virtuosic exfoliation of nested chronicles that give voice to the heterogeneous temporalities that make for "the people." This is a maximalist poetics. **RODRIGO TOSCANO**

Good morn or evening, friends. . . . This book is ravishing and ravaging, and/or wants to be, which is troubling, though that is as it should be. Can we dream ourselves inside out of what consumes and abandons us? This question, which bears the world's disaster, is our nightmare, though we are starving, even abandon having been tainted. Projection, ingestion, rejection and introjection merge in the mirror of constantly midnight, brutally Christian profligacies of diary, conquest, denial and refreshment. iles ahead, and just getting started. **FRED MOTEN**

Edgar Garcia comes through with a counter-chronicle of conquest. He shows us how skins are like masks the poet and storyteller puts on and off, most especially when engaged with epic histories and the myths therein, changing places, changing times, and of course, changing us.
**MICHAEL TAUSSIG**

**WINNER OF THE FENCE MODERN POETS SERIES**

*FENCE* publishes with the support of individuals, organizations, and institutions. A not-for-profit corporation, *Fence* is mandated by its board to make decisions unaligned with the requirements of market force or capital concern, and only in with its mission

TO MAINTAIN A DEDICATED VENUE, IN PRINT, AURAL, AND DIGITAL FORMS, FOR WRITING THAT SPEAKS ACROSS GENRE, SOCIO-CULTURAL NICHES, AND IDEOLOGICAL BOUNDARIES, AS ACCESSIBLY AS POSSIBLE SUCH THAT FENCE PUBLISHES LARGELY FROM ITS UNSOLICITED SUBMISSIONS, AND IS COMMITTED TO THE LITERATURE AND ART OF QUEER WRITERS AND WRITERS OF COLOR. FENCE ENCOURAGES COLLECTIVE APPRECIATION OF VARIOUSNESS BY SHOWCASING WRITING THAT INHERES COLLECTIVELY OUTSIDE OF THE CONSTRAINTS OF OPINION, TREND, AND MARKET.

# FENCE

WELCOMES TAX-DEDUCTIBLE DONATIONS,
AND WILL USE THEM TO PAY CONTRIBUTORS.
PLEASE CONSIDER ADDING YOUR SUPPORT
FOR OUR WRITERS. CONTACT THE EDITOR
WITH IDEAS OR QUESTIONS, OR DONATE
ONLINE AT FENCEPORTAL.ORG/SUPPORT.

REBECCAFENCE@GMAIL.COM

# CONTENTS

REBECCA WOLFF
ZINE DESIGN BY REBECCA BORRER

# Happy Marina Abramovic Day Parade

#DisplaceYourself

I wrote this political screed last Columbus Day weekend, 2017, and have suppressed it ever since.
It feels didactic, it feels patronizing, it feels like an unwieldy weapon in something
 that is not a battle but a group-think experiment.
We should be experimenting right now with how to change our reality,
like they did back in the previous days of communes and other Utopian possibilities.
I hope those experiments are happening now, but I feel certain at the same time that they are not enough.
Here in gentrifying Hudson we should be leveraging ourselves as human cannonballs
 from within the walls of this walled city.

We are inside of it, it is our reality,
and we owe it to ourselves and to our neighbors to create our own reality.

This zine you hold in your hands constitutes a shared reality, and a token of my love
for what I will claim as my community. Twenty years ago I took on the role of publisher
as a reformer of the kind of localized representation of art in literature (this means
books without spines) that cannot be easily sold in bookstores but must instead be passed
hand to hand—that in my view bred a combined provincialism and inaccessibility;
keeping "bad" or regressive art in; withholding privileged views of secretive
avant gardisms—a stew of circumscription. Over these twenty years
I have been educated as to the pleasures and mercies of boundaries.
It turns out I just never before cared enough about a community, literary or otherwise,
to wish to speak directly to it.

# #DISPLACE YOURSELF

Rebecca Wolff

Artist Citizens of Hudson, NY:

If you understand art, then you understand metaphor, and you also might understand states of extremity.

You will be able to understand how the art-strike that I am calling for functions as a metaphor:

for a call to do commit yourself to concrete action, large or small or in-between, that will

advance the various causes of generationally poor, low-income people of color living in Hudson.


Columbus Day was already three weeks ago.

My children wondered whether there would be a parade on Warren Street.

I assured them there would not, and that furthermore there could not be a better time—when the whole nation,

aside from about half of it, is awake to the wrongheadedness of celebrating a murderous and rapacious takeover

of a once great and beautiful land mass, upon which we might all have thrived but instead now are dying

senselessly in great number, poisoned by our opportunities and industries—to re-cast this holiday in a different light.


Who among us does not now understand that Christopher Columbus,

and the hordes of land-grabbers and empire-builders who came subsequently to "develop"

the continent, are to be reprimanded, rather than celebrated, for their actions

and the crimes against not only humanity, human lives erased in the quest for capital gain,

but also against nature, and the glorious structures she had erected already,

mountains and rivers

and lakes and forests and plains?

Swamps and oceans, lagoons and gulfs and

aeries and ponds?

It is possibly neither accident nor coincidence that on the same weekend that Columbus Day was proclaimed dead

in the city of Detroit, another explorer, Marina Abramovic, chose to announce her "abandonment" of Hudson.

I was but one of many citizens present six years or so ago at the press conference she held

in the still-vacant Community Tennis court to unveil her scale-model of the museum of durational conceptual performance

and, more expansively, her plans for the city of Hudson to become an art tourism mecca.

She leveled one clear demand: Build More Hotels.

I also remember Marina's response to a query from the public, a soft ball as it were,

regarding how she thought the opening of this museum might affect the lives of the existing residents of Hudson.

She stated:


## "I haven't thought about that."


Or words to that effect.


In early 2018, at one of new Mayor Rick Rector's conversational meeting for citizens in the First Ward

I was encouraged at his statements of openness to solutions and desire for further conversation,

ongoing throughout his impending tenure as Mayor, a durational performance

of a different kind than Marina may have curated, but with assuredly just as much potential impact

on citizens of Hudson's quality of life for decades to come. At that meeting Rick Rector said these words out loud:


## "There is nothing you can do to stop gentrification."


Or words to that effect.

Artists of Hudson: Do not celebrate Christopher Columbus; and do not celebrate Marina Abramovic either.

Do not arrive in a place and think that you can do whatever you want to it or with it. You are not the first ones here.

# You did not discover Hudson.

Hudson is a city; it has a citizenry and a populace and an infrastructure.

Do not come here and open an art space when by doing so you are genuinely accelerating the firestorm of gentrification

that is displacing people of color and low income people just as effectively as a wild fire in California,

a real one or a fictional one, created not by god but by human inattention

and the devious and explicit diversion of political engagement into artist's statements.

Do not come here in complicity, and make or curate community-based art and fail to integrate your actual body,

the part of you that walks the streets and uses the amenities and lives under a roof, with the other bodies.

Do not come here and think that you are just a cog in a giant machine,

or that there is nothing you can do about the inevitable gentrification process in which you are a helpless ant-worker.

In a city as small as Hudson there is practically a one-to-one relationship between

Someone Making Art and Someone Forced Out. Take advantage of that relationship. Relate to it.

# #DISPLACE YOURSELF

Artists are the carriers of the disease of gentrification.

It is living within your body and you must kill or sacrifice or freeze

some part of yourself in order to halt or reduce its spread.

#YeahDisplaceYourself

Gentrification relies on artists.

Stop making art, curating art, selling art, buying art.

The city is choked with gentrification.

You are not helpless. Take your intelligence and commitment and put it where it matters critically right now.


If your livelihood is selling art,

you probably have enough money to make it through a year without making any more money.

If your livelihood is making art: ditto.

If you feel that you don't have enough money to make it through a year,

consider whether you may be spending more than your share of money.

The median annual household income in Hudson, NY, is

## $33,250

I challenge everyone making art, selling art, curating art, making art-space,

or otherwise making art happen to a two-fold program:


1) **Cease production of consumables—including socially mediated production of yourselves;**

2) **Divert those energies to local political actions that shore up**

**the lives of the people who lived here before you got here.**


Common Council meeting happens every month. Primary day is coming in June.

Find candidates to support in the coming local, state, and national elections and work to get those candidates elected.

Find a Get Out the Vote initiative and work for it. Don't do it in the weeks before the election;

## do it now.

We throw the word "literally" around so ruthlessly these days

that I feel quite confident making this proposal with no further caveat than to say that I mean every word I say.

**For every day that you make or curate or sell art,
take a day to make or directly support political action in Hudson.**

This is kind of like reparations.

I throw the word "artist" around and I throw the word "complicity" around too.

I am an artist and I am complicit.

I have my days of engagement and I have my days of retraction and self-absorption

and requirements for withdrawal and for freedom, or the illusion of it.

As an artist, I also know it's hard to remember that you are just one of many, but you are.

Attend the Hudson City Common Council meeting.

You will be amazed at what kinds of decisions are made in that room, in those meetings,

which then affect the fabric of your reality and of your neighbors.

As an artist you create your own reality,

except when it is created for you by the government.

#YeahDisplaceYourself

You may be thinking: But that's preposterous.

It's already happened, done, over,

and plus no one cares what art is happening in Hudson, NY;

as long as there's pretty old buildings where "creatives" can drape textiles

and airbnb superhosts can stage artisan objet,

the process will continue apace.


I would still offer this challenge.


You may not fully understand the fragility of the security of the citizens;

and commensurately you may not fully understand

how immediately felt are the actions of any person

(especially a person with the agency it takes to make art)

when that agency is applied to the political process.


**Just because you're an artist doesn't mean you have to be a tool.**

Happy Marina Abramovic Day Parade.

# EDGAR GARCIA

FROM *Skins of Columbus*
*winner of the Fence Modern Poets Series*

The journal dreamt itself. Its pages you wrote to capture mental colony from its root in the name, Cristóbal Colón. But what captivities does the name, that sound—*Colón*—hide? Drop its diacritic and you drift like plastic in a sea of erotogenic marks. How does the large intestine entwine in the same sign that names the colon: punctuation preceding explanation, dramatizing the experience of figures and forms? What does a colon do, actually? To explain: what follows is a book whose poems examine the inner workings of colonial myth. To explore the burrowing of our colonial myths into real-life experience—wet violence in the tough skin of emblems and instincts—the author spent four months reading the journal of Christopher Columbus before sleep. Later, he transformed his dreams into a poetic record of what his memory, in its half-sleep, had forgotten it remembered: the gash, shock, glamour, void, punctuation, and spell of origins. It belonged to that history as intimately as that history belonged to the momentary constellations of a night sky. Its belonging, unclear and unassimilated, anacoluthic but self-instructive, is the shining of dark stars equipped with consciousness.

To say simply that you could subvert Columbus and the world he left us only stages the inadequacy of the curse to do away with the accursed object. As usual, reality is contrary. The curse imprecates the curser, the interdict awakens the nightmare, iconoclasts are slaves of icons, and, critical truisms though these may be, you conjure yourself inside them constantly: to subvert is to crumble to the enterprise of memory overturned, to hurl body over the head of mental colony only to flip back upward, part to an assed whole. So the question, for you at least, is how to flip from realities different than those of the colonial myth—how to stay true to the reality of myth, which bakes the crust of your thought with its hot white light, while hitching somehow to new suns and ideas. How do you look inside yourself for its terrible illumination while shedding new light on that light? Could you, with mirror or sword-face even for an instant, blind the gods and their higher powers?

To be clear: you are not looking for wisdom, but for a world unfolding in dreams. In October 2015, soon after moving to Chicago, you came up with a strategy for this. You came to it while browsing the yearly Hyde Park Used Book Sale, which takes place on Columbus Day weekend. In the chaotic pile of 30,000 books separated into fifty sections in Dole, Del Monte, and Chiquita produce boxes—emanations of the United Fruit Company—you came across a hardcover edition of Bartolomé de las Casas's sixteenth-century *Journal of Christopher Columbus*. Reading the entry for that day, the 10th, there amid the boxes and browsing shoppers, you saw the rain chop the waves, shake the whole history from inside out, and take you into the storm pulling his ship down the sea. In two days, he would see land. But, at that moment, he was in the darkest kind of sleep. So you decided to awaken with him, to see if you could see what your mind saw in what he saw and, in doing so, to flash a mirror into the beach-boiled eye of the unsleeping colonial sun.

That night, and every night for the next three months during which he traveled the coasts, tricking history into his tasks, you read the journal before bed closely to have your sleeping mind think intently on its images, plots, symbols, motives, and feelings. You wished to see what, when left to its matrix of associations, your mind made of the colonial story. Notes throughout the night recorded your dreams. In the mornings, you made new notations to chart closer contacts between you two, dreamer and traveler. You composed the text in the evenings, putting your dreams and the journal together into a new story of creation. What you made you now hold in your hands: the positions, spaces, and temporalities of history are tasks you gave yourself, entanglements warped in a historical structure that depends on you for its unfolding churn, which discloses itself in both nights and days. Here is a study about how language is captivated by and captures the negativity of the hemispheric experience surging from its southern sources—how its inconsistency and unevenness are stopgaps because in practice a body and its myth are not exclusive of each other, but reciprocal and dynamic, semiotic and aesthetic. These are signs and the instances in which they unravel themselves. Like a first being looking out from the gauzy green light of a newborn cosmos, you saw the gods then as so many cascading storms.

Sunday/Thursday, October 11th

Roughest sea so far tube-nosed seabirds
on green reeds a cane a stick bobbing
carved iron and a small board with marks
like lizard hands
like little lights at the end of a hall
signaling pigs to squeal hopes of land

through day we landed and saw
the lizards upright like sideways
Fs or Ys upside-down
crimping their necks to look at us
impossible words by force by
fish chopping the water around us all

My Christ, my surrendering fish
I see what you signal:
To take the dinosaurs by force

Tuesday/Saturday, October 13th

To a broken planet came men
bellies and long hair, carved like
spears all wet all playing games

They are a pleasure to watch
so flat so slender so fast they

split my world in two into
a dead body hiding in my skin

Wednesday/Sunday, October 14th

The island sick fearful shouts to us
coming from heaven for help to us

Thursday/Monday, October 15th

Anchor daylight free from shoals
Hoisted sails, bracelets, legs, and arms
Crystals the shape of diamonds
I touched to make them shudder &
look away & I could take what I want

bracelets on their arms and legs
in their ears noses
and around their necks plus
some dry sliced leaves they prize

Friday and Saturday/Tuesday and Wednesday, October 16th

watching an airplane crash feels like
Is like what I feel watching their canoes
off the coast subtending
Making wobbly half-circles inside me
Bags of human shit hanging from my lungs
I don't know how to describe it
The explosive fire across the water
Have you ever seen a plane crash?
I haven't. But I fear what it feels like
Seeing all those people dip down

# Mattilda Bernstein Sycamore

## A Desert Island

One problem with gentrification is that it always gets worse.

But then I go into a Hooters, and it's a vintage clothing store. A friend of mine is trying on breasts. This is why I like dreaming.

I remember when faggots kissed hello. We had so much to fear and so we feared nothing, I mean we feared one another but we feared fear more. Kissing one another on the lips, this was joyous and commonplace, a legacy we were inheriting, an art—how to stretch out our lips in front our faces, how to queen it up in front of a loving or hostile public, how to emphasize connection or disdain.

We kissed hello because we had to. We had to know we could kiss like this, a simple greeting but something splendid and transgressive even when mundane, or that's what it felt like for me when I moved to San Francisco in 1992, and I was 19. This kiss didn't necessarily feel like a radical act, it was just something you did if you were a faggot, whether in suit and tie or broadcasting the pageantry of outsider imagination. Was this something that united us? I wouldn't have said so then, but maybe I'm saying it now.

Yes, there were the ones who turned their cheeks, too good for this kiss unless they explained the sudden turn by mentioning a cold sore, one just starting or one in the past, whichever way we hoped we were taking care. Sometimes you knew someone had really bad breath, but you kissed her on the lips anyway, it was okay to endure a little discomfort to avoid seeming snotty or scared. Unless this was one of those queens who would grab you and start feeling you up, that was a good reason to avoid contact.

You kissed the ones you loved and the ones you didn't even like that much, sometimes even someone you hated, just so you wouldn't seem shady. Too much garlic was never a problem, we kissed anyway. We kissed the living and the dying, knowing that the dying were part of the living and we wanted to keep them with us.

Maybe this was a dream—I mean I know it wasn't a dream then, but maybe it is now. Now we're more afraid, afraid of one another, so even the gestures of intimacy disappear. Most of the time I don't even think of kissing someone hello anymore, I reach for a hug if possible and this can be beautiful too, but in a different way. How strange to think that in the early-'90s, when it felt like everyone was dying, we were less fearful in certain ways.

When I'm washing my hair in the shower, and suddenly I think what the hell am I doing? Oh, I'm in the shower—this is one of the things I do in the shower. Sometimes repetition leads to revelation, and sometimes revelation leads to repetition, which leads to no revelation ever again.

You know when you notice someone's looking at you, but you're not sure, so you do the same thing you were just doing, so you don't look like you're looking? I was holding a piece of chewed-up licorice root in front of my face in between two fingers, getting ready to throw it out the window. He lit a cigarette. I hate cigarettes, but that's the place for them, downstairs and outside and away from my window. He crossed the street, looked back, waited, so then I literally leaned out the window. He came back. Eventually I said do you want to come up? And he did. That's when I knew my life could start again.

There's a certain kind of knowledge, growing up in a particular body, socialized to be a particular thing you will never be, knowing this and learning to grow with it instead of against. Maybe I'm saying we all need different kinds of people in our lives, right? When anything becomes homogenous, there's a problem. When anything becomes so homogenous that people don't even think about it, that's worse.

I used to live in a neighborhood where no one belonged, and so we all belonged. Now I live in a neighborhood where faggots look at me like I don't belong, and so I don't. Soon they won't belong either, but this won't make anything better.

There's too much desire without desire. Too much desire for desire. Not enough desire. Sometimes we remember the dead, and forget the living dead. And sometimes we forget everything. We make art so we don't die. And still we die. Silence is a kind of memory, but memory should never be a form of silencing. Maybe there are exceptions. I know a process can be collective, and a collective can be in-process, but what about a collective process without collective process?

Knowing the gap between what you want and what you yearn for, can there be hope in this? Maybe I'm saying that yearning often comes from spurning, the brokenness from that glance, the desire for seamlessness. Maybe there's no way not to be broken, only a way not to feel broken.

But then I actually make the move, first my leg close to his, then my hand a friendly brush against his cheek, eventually we're making out and this is when my brain can relax. Maybe not just my brain but everything. This is what it means to have a body.

The conversation is important because it's not important. This is what people do at bars.

At some point he asks me where I live. His name's Caleb. I ask him if he wants to come home with me. He says: I'm undetectable.

Where's the transition, I mean it's like he's online. I guess some people are always online.

I say I'm negative. He asks me if I fuck raw, he says he wants to fuck my brains out. I say no, I use condoms—but we don't have to fuck, there are lots of other things we can do.

The truth is that I wasn't even thinking about fucking, I just wanted to continue the way this was making me feel. He says no it's not going to work out.

But still I'm here, in my body. I want to be here. I want to be here, in my body. With him. You're adorable, he says, later, when he's back and we're making out again.

Adorable—I love that word.

He asks me where I live again. I guess he's that drunk.

He yells over at some guy who just arrived: I wanna fuck the shit out of you.

I remember a phone sex ad from 2001, with someone who looked just like this other guy, pretending to be a gas station attendant with rhinestone studs in his ears and jeans with textured pockets. We can't always be attracted to people we don't immediately think are tragic. The way my heart stops a little and I feel the sensation of not moving. But why? I don't want anyone to fuck my brains out.

Caleb says let's switch positions, so now I'm next to James, who makes clothes. He likes my clothes. Maybe Caleb wants me to go home with James, is this strange or kind or a little bit of both I'm not sure but I like James too.

This is what happens at bars, or can happen, if you're lucky.

James says do you live in Seattle? Because I've never seen you around. And I say that's because I don't go out. So he wants to know why.

Somehow I feel so comfortable, even though I'm wondering what this comfort means, how I could feel comfortable in this world where I don't exist anymore, a world I've fled, a world that rarely welcomes me, a world I need so fucking badly or maybe I'm not thinking all of this yet. I say I don't go out because of the smoke, even smoke machines—because I don't drink—and because I deal with a lot of chronic health problems.

I'm worried about being too serious, here at this table with these fags I've just met, you're not supposed to be too serious at bars.

But how do Caleb and I end up in the bathroom together, I guess it's after he shows me a picture of his dick on his phone, I mean he says it's an accident but I'll take foreplay any way I can get it so we're making out against the wall by the toilet and then he's pushing me downward so I'm on my knees, yes, his dick in my mouth, someone comes in and maybe Caleb's ready to pull away, but I could stay here all night. Then we're in the bathroom that locks, he smacks my face kind of hard and I love it—how could this sex already feel so connected, now he's sucking my cock, pulling on my nipples, but then I say that's too hard, rub my chest, and then he does it right.

I ask him if he wants me to smack his face too, he doesn't, somehow this is kind

7

of funny and then he stands up and says that was your chance.

My chance for what?

Your chance to get off.

I didn't know I was trying to get off.

Later, he's telling me I'm adorable again, I really do love that word. He leaves to go home, but then he's back, and he looks really sad.

I start to say did you just have a mood swing, but I stop myself because maybe that's too familiar. What happened, I say, and he says it's nothing, I just missed the bus.

I say I just got really sad because you're sad, is that okay?

Are we making out, or just petting each other, or am I just petting him—he's adorable, is that okay to say, even while he's sad? Do you see how I'm so present? How this presence can mean so much, even in a situation that really means nothing.

He doesn't want my number, I already know that. He has a boyfriend. Everyone in the bar is smashed because this is Sunday night, Sunday night early but early Sunday night is the messiest. This is why people are hooking up in the bathroom, this is why people are being honest, at least some of the people, but I like it even if it's the messiness that makes people more open—I don't need it but maybe they do. Beneath the shade and the shame and the sadness, there's a sweetness, and I haven't felt this in years I mean have I ever.

So I'm walking home with James, I mean he's walking to the next bar and I'm walking him there on my way home. Everyone was exchanging stories at the bar, so I ask him if it's okay to talk about Caleb, does Caleb always get sad like that, is he a sad drunk?

We talk about what we do, whatever that means but there's a connection I think, I mean I need to come back into the world, maybe even this world. I kiss James goodbye, I mean we kiss goodbye, and I make it into the kiss that means we're making out until he indicates with his hands that that's enough and then we say we'll get together soon. This is a part of me that I want to be part of, I mean I want this back. How long it's been since I've had fag friends in my daily life. How much longer it's been since I've dated anyone I mean over a decade. What my body needs in order to be a body that's not just a body of needs. I'm getting really emotional. I'm right at the edge of being able to cry.

When I get home, the phone is ringing and I see that it's James, he's calling to give me his number because he forgot that he already gave me his number. I feel like I'm back in my body and I'm shut down. I'm so close to crying. Somewhere there's a place in my body where I can actually feel alive.


Walking through Tashkent in the morning and doesn't that sound romantic, but really it's just the name of a tiny park of dirt and dogshit—someone comes rushing up to me and says I hope this doesn't sound weird, but I saw you on the bus the other day, and I really like the way you dress. He looks like the awkward best friend from one of those movies in the '80s except he was probably born in the '90s—in a month he's flying to Bangkok to travel through Southeast Asia because he doesn't know what he's doing with his life.

And then, as I'm getting closer to the real park, Volunteer, I mean I like everything about this park except its name in honor of the volunteers in the Spanish-American War, the way colonialism is always there, even when we're looking at the trees and just as I'm about to enter the park I hear someone saying hell-lo! I look over, and there's an older woman with curly gray hair in a sleek silver car, slowing down to stop the car behind her, and I figure she's going to ask for directions, but instead she says **YOU. LOOK. FABULOUS.**

And then I get a rush through my body, this is what I'm looking for, this feeling of feeling what's going on inside, me, and then at the end of the walk, when I'm getting closer to home, tired now, looking in at the yoga boutique to see a black tank top with shiny copper lettering that says, wait, already I can't remember, one of those yoga slogans, fill in the blank, next to tie-dye print hotpants, and a blue sweatshirt reading **LOVE IS ALL YOU NEED,** because really all you need is this sweatshirt.

When you wonder what you've always wondered but in a different way, maybe this is what it means to grow. To move into a new space of wondering.

I want my body to feel my body. I want my body to feel.

Sometimes I feel invisible, which is not the same thing as saying I am invisible. I'm leaving Volunteer Park again, at the end of another morning walk. Some guy's following me in his car, but I'm kind of in denial about it because it's the middle of the day. And, because I'm wearing a purple hat with a flower on it—faggots are so afraid of flowers. Probably he's straight.

I have a private garage, he says, before driving me into a building where every parking spot is taken. I need to piss. He opens the door to a stairwell—you can piss here, no one ever uses this stairwell. What do you like to do, he says, and I don't have the answer because I'm attracted to the dynamic, but not to him. First of all, way too much cologne.

He wants to fuck me, which sounds pretty hot in this stairwell with the unfinished stairs and cement floor, but he doesn't have a condom. We can go next door, he says, RiteAid, which isn't next door.

I say we can go to my place, and when we get inside he starts to sit on my bed and I say don't sit there, I'm pretty sensitive to cologne, I hope that's okay. Of course he has poppers, even though he says he wasn't looking for sex. He fucks me on the floor in the entryway, maybe not the best thing for my knees. When he's done, he throws the condom in the toilet. Luckily he doesn't flush. He says are you shy, you seem pretty shy.

But I might have just been invited to a covert Super Bowl party. I keep listening to the message to see if it says we will be watching football, or we won't. There's something about making vegan curry, but do you think it's a trap? What if I get there, and everyone's wearing Seahawks helmets and cock-socks?

Suddenly it's very quiet. I guess I should go outside while the game is going on, and then get back home before it ends, right? Sudden memories of my father screaming at the TV. He thought that if he screamed loud enough, this would make him working-class—just one of the guys, getting drunk in front of the TV. A working-class psychiatrist.

I don't know which is worse, people who watch football because they like football, or people who watch because everyone else is watching.

Now I'm in another gay bar. I knew it would be awful, but I didn't know it would be this awful.

When someone asks WHAT'S YOUR REAL NAME, you might be in the wrong place. When four different people ask WHAT'S YOUR REAL NAME, you're definitely in the wrong place.

Then there's the queen who says are you a boy or a girl—JUST KIDDING!!! People at gay bars have really evolved.

This queen was dating someone who had my haircut, he was 25 and she thought he really liked her, but then he said she was too feminine. And short.

I am short, she says.

She doesn't like it when people say how old are you, what a ridiculous question. Then she says: How old are you?

She had sex with one of the barbacks, but she didn't like it when he said he usually likes to fuck several guys in a row. They were at a bathhouse.

Every gay bar is an accidental comedy routine. The best comedy routine is the one that takes itself seriously.

When you see a sign in the bathroom that says ANYONE CAUGHT SELLING OR USING DRUGS WILL BE BANNED FROM THIS ESTABLISHMENT, you know where to find drugs.

When someone in the bathroom says I've never been pee-shy before in my entire life—is this a compliment? I end up watching the guys playing pool in the room that isn't so overheated, drunken hipsters humping the table, kind of out of place in this bar where the suburban imagination hasn't even caught on to hipsterism. The hottest one for me is kind of butch but he's wearing this T-shirt with little flowers on it—I'm in love with that T-shirt, I mean I'm in love with that T-shirt on him. He comes over to introduce himself and when I hold out my hand he does that thing like he's confused that I'm not offering a proper masculine handshake, but somehow I don't mind because I like the feeling of his hand so much. He keeps looking at me, and later he says he's going outside to smoke but he'll be back, so I lean over to kiss him, just to be friendly but also to see what might happen and what happens is that he turns away and reaches for my hand again. But I don't need another handshake so I kiss his neck—what matters is that I've gone up to the one I'm most attracted to, I've gone up and I've made a move and now it's time for me to go home.

Suddenly remembering all those times when I reached my hand out for someone to crush me. But without mandatory masculinity, what would I be? I still remember that cactus I threw out the window as a kid when it poked me, and then it just grew and grew. When I say hi, my name's Mattilda, and everything's not already over. That sounds so basic. I mean it is so basic. I can't remember the last time someone asked what I would do if I was stuck on a desert island.

Before I threw the cactus out the window, I found a worm on the sidewalk, and I was playing with it, pressing a stick into its squishy body to see which way it would move—I pressed a little harder, and it split in half. So then there were two worms. Was this possible? They were still moving around. Until I realized that worm was dead. I had killed it. I didn't want to kill anything ever again. I watched the ants building their cities, wondering what I looked like to them.

The difficulty of translation is the translation of difficulty. This city that is and isn't a city, but I guess that's what every city is becoming now, a destination to imagine what imagination might be like, except for the lack. Some terrible things are worse than other terrible things, but this doesn't mean we need more terrible things.

Sometimes going to the grocery store makes me feel less alone. Sometimes I'm trying to tell someone about this new opening in my life, and I end up feeling closed. When I say opening, I mean the possibility that when I feel I won't feel like I shouldn't feel. My body in a room with other bodies feeling me feeling my body. When I say this room I mean you. When I say you I mean make room.

On a good day, I write in sentences. On a bad day, I write in thoughts. You know when you're dreaming, and past and present blend together in a way that makes it feel like maybe you can imagine a future? And then you wake up.

# TESS BROWN-LAVOIE

## *Always To Do*

There is a landscape I return to once I've been let down by every last body. Not a horizon, but a fully fleshed out three dimensions— with the topography of a furrowed brow— my gaze is the unadulterated sun ready to burn skin. My papers— technology— sobriety— and intoxication. After the second heartbreak I called my desperate list: ALWAYS TO DO. Snap back to my personal pleasure texture™ with a change in body temperature, submersion in water, or words: that letter— reservoir dive— riverside run. Started from the bottom and now it seems I am poised to pay less in taxes than I did last year.

I may have systematically compromised my hire-ability by not giving a fuck. Dad cautions be careful about what you put out there— on the internet e.g.— which he should have thought of before idolizing David Bowie in front of me. Honesty is a person's own treasure. She protects it when she is at war. She is generous when she can be.

The oral steroid has me susceptible to oscillations in mood. Small lies bother me— my persona is lost in a sea of jobs— violence proceeds throughout the city. Days do not end— my friends are under institutional scrutiny— racist appointees hold their hands to our inspired tyrant— the solar eclipse left us mad.

Dismiss upset as a severe teacher would. Despair wears the face of every new person I love. Forever shift between desires— solitude and dependence— unfold the list and identify a neutral act. Fold laundry, always. Always read a devotional text. Bathe. Anoint with whatever oil. Burn an herb, any local herb.

I asked for a sign knowing full well I wouldn't recognize its appearance. I prayed. You know what— a sign was sent. As a book, actually— a novel, with its inanimate guarantee: 200 pages of good company. Sustained attention. The generosity of its preparation— development— the physical act of typing it even— devotion over time— my most poignant reference point for the idea of marriage. From the couch, the promise of literature furnished momentum to open a reluctant emotional door. After functional days on end, I finally put away the cleaning supplies— crossed the polished threshold. This being the first time the full house was ever mopped.

Back within the interior thanks to the holy book. Optimized despite underachieving in the sleep department. Please consider Sunday for the most valuable player award. Things will be sad and complex forever— I surrender to fiction; the dispersoned to-do list supersedes selfhood. Just bobbing in a galaxy where the force of gravity is directly proportional to the intensity of my focus. The generosity of libraries moves me.

When I learned the vocabulary word miser in middle school, I pictured a very different man than me. I smile sometimes and will give it away to a stranger at no charge. But save the fine slice for myself— the most gratifying moment— a carry-on suitcase full of secrets— that I will never divulge— or only if my judgment is compromised— rent open by dentist drugs. I will bury the secrets bestowed to me in inscrutable text— ornamented and sealed like ancient royals in their tombs.

Trolls out there defy ethics. There are colossal repercussions to honesty, is what my dad and the news said. He prays for one single peaceful day— and knows a little something about losing almost everything, including his ALWAYS TO DO list. Sometimes the least life-ruining act is leaving the land line off the hook while haywire functions reset and recalibrate. If this seems vague in a poetry type of way, it is and is not. I'm comparing the breakdown of a human resources department with very clinical ruptures. That young child mediator tends to reproduce the new chaos I live and write today.

When all the inputs pile on one another, it seems the only thing to do is find somebody else to tell me what to do for once. You heard right: seeking a boss w4w.

A ripe prince saddles the Honda and speeds north. My Element. Ask how I will be trained, how I will be valued, what aspirations, what client, the gradient of my personas. It is useful to externalize these questions.

When a pop star rips off her tuxedo to reveal a bathing suit shaped costume, that is an escalation. Generally a tuxedo ups the ante, but a bikini is a trump card in almost any setting. This moment calls for a different transitional outfit. Something like pajamas in disguise. Some kind of robe that keeps personal contours under wraps. Fashion hair is only as sustainable as one's patience with regime.

My suit is hearts— cups— and my earthly vessel gilded. With capacity for full or emptiness— with a functional pulse. My element is water— my Honda is hose-able— the qualities of liquid I relate to include that it takes the vessel's shape— that it freezes in conditions of cold— that its vapors penetrate the caves behind one's face— that its molecules subdivide into ions, positive or otherwise.

When darkness is incomplete clouds absorb street light like a couch in the rain. Tonight anxiety is matte. A desperate earplug limits the circumference of my mind to the inside of my skull. In New Hampshire I got a lamp for a quarter; that lamp is tonight's midnight oil. Arrange a pillow. Take whatever medicine. Hysterical prose. Anticipating sleep with nothing between the two of us but a book.

## Post Script

The time between my last word and your unwritten one is a footprint that fills with mud. I am raising pigs for slaughter, and their affinity for mud affects my use of the image. I have new mud reverence, its sounds and cooling properties.

I would be a nun without you, and wish you would not exist. At my best I write selfishly, archeologist of private vocabulary. Gentle with my brush so as to not disturb the bones and porcelain as they lie. You are the repository. The outdoors— rain catchment system. I water my garden. A vine grows into the negative shape of unresponsiveness. I am that invasive species— the opportunistic rhizome with fervor to extremely cover ground. I am becoming unreadable. I don't care if your attention is adequate. You are not necessary after all, not in this present incarnation as the penpal equivalent of a fuckboy.

This exchange has turned into a bit of a squash game— I make a vigorous gesture, my content bounces geometrically off a wall. I liked when you were the rock formation my river encountered, but now you are truly rocklike: my content pours across the floodplain of you. My implicit: splintering in the echo chamber of non-response. I'm not upset this time. I wish to be gentle— as I am not always— and also direct about my purpose. Do you mind? It does not matter if you do. I thought you were responsible for the loudness in me, but even without you I am a screamer. The answer about the tree in the forest is obviously that it does make a magnificent sound.

## FAQ on the Divine Mercy Part Two

Religious forum genre is special, very holy writing. People share profound feelings, and can be philosophers any day of the week. Some more topics we discuss together include:

> *Newbie question about the 54 day Rosary*
> *Praying for those who do not believe in Jesus Christ*
> *What's the Proper Way to Dispose of Sacred Material*
> *Was St. Cyprian a Donatist?*
> *Does God Exist????*
> *Did C. S. Lewis have a known view on Catholicism*
> *New*
> *Is it acceptable to take matters into your own hands if*
>    *authorities will not enforce the law?*
> *Contraception isn't exactly sinful outside of marriage…*
> *Deuterocanonical books?*
> *Please pray for my mom.*
> *FAQ on The Divine Mercy*
> *Not supposed to pray for your own personal peace?*

You know how a seashore is considered a tempting place to relax? Does it get to anyone else that there is unrelenting tension in the shifting tide? Just the other day I left my clothes on dry sand, went naked to submerge, and returned to find the salt water trying on my boots.

It is wrong to blame water. Who hasn't stolen boots or rendered outfits unwearable when overcome by oceanic sensation?

Other people's boyfriends call me a witch. The hot legacy of my birthplace— incessant hero's journey advice dispensed through periodic bursts of clinical or quotidian mania— sexism— just needs somewhere to hang its coat. Almost a genetic predisposition— latent power between shoulder blades, between constellations, I don't even know. My special evil is broad and right as the ocean.

My mother lists places where we lived through the "best of times/worst of times" period a family might review in a nostalgic way following a somewhat alleviated condition of poverty. I have only one memory of Lenox, Mass— a cartoon composite in which all the woodland creatures gather placid before the window in a cute tableau: deer, possum, raccoon, fox, mouse, turtle, rabbit, frog. Laura: "did you recall we hand-fed them hot dogs?"

It is 100% certain my first memory never happened per se. Memory-wash it in the whirlpool washing machine til it is dizzy as a philosopher. My vast ocean. Inland appliance. Geography of salt water laced to the moon.

Respond to this question if you're a forum gal seeking spiritual fulfillment:

*Does God Exist????*

PonderingJak rationalizes:

*The last three days I spent stuck in a motor home watching my two brothers at an American Heritage Girls camp. I am 14, they are 4 and 9. They weren't there most of the time (off having fun most of the time, turns out I wasn't needed or wanted) and I mostly spent my time reading a single picture book of Doctor Who and watching movies picked by the younger kids. I became bored very quickly and soon took to thinking about my religion. Lately, life has sucked, and has ever since I started trying to get more involved with my faith. Turns out, life was actually fun beforehand. And as I sat and thought, I realized that religion seemed like something to pacify and calm down people. And over time, whenever someone pointed out a flaw, they were quickly shushed and sent away. The questions they raised were given rational answers and dismissed. And the main reason that I thought this was because everything seems too perfect. People scared of dying? It's all right, after they do, they'll go to heaven if they've been good and spend eternity having fun. Bad things happen? Oh, it's all part of "God's Plan" and everything will turn out okay. And if it doesn't? You'll end up dying and going to heaven, so nothing bad there. You have no idea what to do? Offer your suffering to God. That's one of the things I don't get. You shouldn't "blame" other people for things. You shouldn't pass off your problems to other people. But it's okay because there's a being who conveniently can take all of that away. The most convincing thing I've seen is in this link: http://imgur.com/gallery/MAgQWlr. Look at that. It's surrounded by posts that are supposed to be funny, and a whole bunch of idiocy, but this one picture spoke volumes to me. All that wide open space, and there's one tiny planet that apparently is the only thing worth saving. There's a God that cares about that planet, because deep down everyone wants to be cared about, and this goes back to what I was saying earlier: it all seems too perfect. And while this doesn't justify it, please believe me when I say that I had a whole bunch of stuff I thought about that I wanted to put down but mentally can't put up with.*

To which Lion IRC rejoinders:

*I love that God made a huge 'Taj Mahal' universe for us to dwell in. It shows how much He cares for us. If God placed us in a dismal, tiny "shoe box" of a universe that would cause me to doubt His love, His power and His majesty.*

I love that answer. To me that totally explains it.

# LAURA SIMS

## *Walking Dead Love Song 39*

I am done with Walking Dead
says someone
not me
I have no agency

Your valley of wrath
sustains me
coddles me
please do not
wean me I'm
hungry

Your bludgeoning
bat and your
gluttony wasted
the last
good man
on TV

Look the blood
runs around me
colors &
warms me

My little gray cat
sits by the screen
wanting in

He can't see
the squalor &
holiness
in
has been
bringing me

# Eleni Sikelianos

from *What I Knew*

Found a man-body under blankets in Flagstaff down by the creek
where the father's body was once kicking H
frozen, flowering at the chest
his heart was bumped    was hunched and hurt

Were you going to leave him and let the wolves eat him?

Some bodies
can never be found and some
can never be bound

And in Seattle where it always sounds like someone's taking a shower
it smells like dumb luck
in muscular Seattle rooted down in its piney ground

the light is blind
& she is there
Susqually'absh
People of the Grass

       and a brown-haired boy, Highway 5, in the car next-door biting
             into a Subway    vicing    innocent    speeding
       around Puget Sound

I know a small world away from Medicine Creek Treaty     rising    Tumwater and

any river's watershed          plus
Large Americans anywhere
O large Americans, love of

Shoeless in Seattle stress
relief therapy   in the child's poem a potato
falls on the pop
star's head (it's Justin
Bieber's)

I will not
look this up
on the internet               why the blue

portion of white light
from the sun is
               scuzzily  scattered
over Rangoon and Kuching

All I know is blue

And in Colorado I will tell you

          *Crows in the snow*          Hello.
          *Crows in the snow*          Goodbye.

                              (*Hei-hei*, Anselm Hollo)

Also, a crane on the sky-

line glints from the high-

way ,    geese strip across the dinosaur

   cloud loping, skidding behind it

This is a world.  This is a world-

view     /    Happiness every day in America


what we come to know and how we know it

and here I pile all I do or will not know


             "pony," "brake," "star," "oak," "green," "ridge," "tree," "to hide," "to flee"


How do you say Whenever they dance let me see near Sacramento?

The crackling blackbirds behind the words in Pipil?


I don't even know what I am.

Which brings me here.

                    To the god of all my gemstones

                              cracking potent violet flame St. Germaine


In the morning a man with glasses gets

into a car & I think It might be Kenneth Koch because I

am a poet and he is a poet.  But this is not New York & Kenneth Koch


is dead.


The world is poor.

What is poverty?

Mother

I am a rich relation.


I am a poor friend.


Poverty is the bodies
gone into the ground making
the ground rich, she said.


One sack of rich rice         *For goodness sakes, Max*, the blonde
could do what                 mother passing me said.
in the world.


The mind is awake in the twilight    Max is apparently the dog.
a receptive wave
hovering
like a flying saucer in the dim light


a bowl of milk around which
the flies have gathered.


They are fireflies.


What I am I cannot say.



But will tell of all I heard and saw when I was in
an ancient world, holding

tablets of red rock

up to the sea-cave roof to show

we're ancient too, to fit time

back together                    as if


you could reconstruct a broken brain and face

a human world and race

an animal symmetry lounging into the future


in the same way a scarab beetle's blue

has no blue but coils in a peculiar

cellular

twist, like an onion's skin, and light

                                        filters        down

through layers to give structural color, bouncing

back blue   .     That kind

of complexity.        (For kick, fur glow, I know a few other cells do

a few other colors too.)



Saw I radar pulses, freeways, Home Depot, Whole Foods so that everywhere

looked like everywhere else America, yet


Every late

Light returns to its own rewards

And finds itself early once again,

Young,

New,

Enlivened

# LEAH DWORKIN

## *The Usuals*

The multiverse theory is a theory that says there are a billion universes happening at once. This means that in another universe I'm at a lesbian bar snorting lines of fire ants off the antlers of a taxidermied moon-deer, while in another space I am sleeping in a desert under a mosquito net covered with metallic scarab beetles the size of evening bags. Somewhere else, a John hand-feeds me lychee nuts while I bronze beside our infinity pool, and at the same moment, someplace else, I've never learned to make sound. There are other stranger universes, harder to understand, universes where there is no you, no he, no she, no it, no I. But I don't really care about these universes, as I'm here in my bodega, ordering an egg and cheese sandwich from Kazmir, who is my bodega guy.

He begins our ritual. "*You*," he says, then asks "the usual?" so I say "Yup." This morning I'm alone, so Kazmir gives me a batty wink, says you haven't come in here with a man for a while. He's soberly observed my nights out and my morning-afters regularly for the past twelve years, possessing a wider scope of my sexual history than anybody else possibly could, myself included. I have the tendency to delete people, while Kazmir prides himself on an excellent memory. When I'm up at night getting beer with the exceptionally tall bongo player I just met in the bathroom line at *Bembe*, Kazmir is on the night shift grinning at me from behind the perspiring six-pack I've just put on the counter, and in the morning, when I come back with a lopsided Jew-fro and my ex-boyfriend, he's waiting for me at the egg station, spatula in hand.

"Is the hook getting too old and cranky for the fishies to bite?" he asks in his way that's simultaneously flirtatious and paternal. When it comes to his attempts to stretch his shitty English, I've become fluent in translation. Still, I resent being the hook in this confused metaphor. The men are the hooks. I'm the lone trout swimming loops in those unmarked dingy waters, lost in some odd bend along the unpronounceable river, dumbly latching my jaws, time and time again, onto poorly camouflaged bait—whatever wiggles. Worms? That's not why I bite. What I'm hungry for is the hook itself. The barb.

"I quit," I say, rolling my eyes. He's cracking my eggs the way I like them, into a dish, first scraping down the griddle to ward off bacon grease contamination, which is why he is the only bodega man I go to in order to fill this particular need. "Quit again!" he squeals. "You always say you quitting before the next batch is rolling!"

"For real, Kazmi ...these 'men' are all crazy, like legit insane, I just don't have the time for it," I say, though all I have is time. I make lazy air quotes when I say the word 'men' to clarify that I'm using the term only because I don't know what else to call them. I'm unsure if my air quotes translate. Kaz looks like the kind of guy born into a language without quotation marks.

" You NewYorkians, it's always time time time," his last resounding *time* transmutes into one of his abstract stories about how time works differently in his country, a country that is at war. Back in his country, which I've come to know through the bodega, every she as old as me has been married for years. By now I'd be living in a home with my husbands' mother, a tired matron who spends each of her mornings involved with a cabbage head, tenderly peeling off leaf under leaf, stuffing the limp layers into what little dough our family has left to make impoverished breads for supper. Once the pan has been scrubbed clean and the sky has gone black, the wives and the husbands and the husbands' mothers and the children and a random aunt or uncle lay together on the shared floor under the bowing U of their dilapidated ceiling, each dreaming that they might be able to get through a whole dream without it being interrupted by an air raid. In this country, he says, his country, where Kaz has a family and a son he claims has eyes so alive that they glow like the eyes of a moon-lit jackal, love is the only thing that matters. Back in my country Kaz is doing what he's supposed to be doing with the butter; it hisses on the griddle.

I don't say anything, what is there to say, really, so Kazmir turns his back to me, tending to my eggs. There is a sadness in Kazmirs back, I start to feel, it is a back that really misses its son. I turn away to grab a coconut water for later. But also, more genuinely, I turn around to avoid the strangeness of the back, the glaring square of sadness above the knot in his apron string. Good coconut waters are outrageously expensive and it's well in my knowledge that the young Thai coconuts have been harvested by monkey slaves, kidnapped from their parents at birth they spend their shortened lives chained to trees, consistently whipped into clearing entire plantations of coconut groves–but I'll be needing the electrolytes once the hangover kicks in. Just as I'm reaching for the chrome fridge handle there it is: the reflection of my dead ex-boyfriend in the glass refrigerator door that's imprisoning the rows of Snapple bottles.

Two choices. Leave without my sandwich or turn around and face that skin who, based on the reflection in front of me, is close, still canvassed around a version of the moving body that it has spent a lifetime stretching around the grooves of. The John. I turn around to face the skin, but once my eyes greet the flesh I have no choice other than to confront the warm, breathing body of John. "You're supposed to be dead," I say. John laughs because we know he isn't dead. John laughs uncomfortably; we're both well aware that I prefer to pretend that he no longer runs a body capable of strolling in and out of bodegas. When John and I broke up for the last time I made us make a pact, as long as we're offline we're dead to each other. "Too bad the bodega isn't virtual," I say to John who looks back at me with a bewildered—no, a humiliated look on his face. The face shows and knows that its body belongs across the river where John has a village of his own, his own bodega, where his own bodega guy, Muhammed, makes him greasier sandwiches.

"You!" The captured face, brown eyes, say you. His you falls somewhere on the spectrum between nostalgic longing and eternal frustration. "How are you?"

"Hungry." I say it fast, realizing that nostalgic longing and eternal frustration aren't exactly that far apart from one another. "You?" I ask.

"Same," he says. The 'm' especially hoists itself in that nook of sound memory, that tight ball of bone between my jaw and my ear resonates with his 'm'. He used to lullaby me to sleep with a song he had written for me, and that second verse was nothing but long rows of m's, only humming. Now, there is a beautiful moment of silence that holds in it the potential for this conversation to be over, before John does what he always does and impulsively sabotages it.

He starts telling me how his mom "mentioned me the other day," because once upon a time I went apple picking with his family and the photo of us all smiling together in front of a Cortland tree is on his parent's refrigerator. From what I remember of the picture, I'm wearing a pink striped tee shirt holding the fat hand of a man-child I loved once.

"That trip was awful," I say to the stranger in his familiar skin who still seems irritably unfazed by me. "It was nice," he says, like we're not even from the same universe. Something vibrates. He whips it out, looks into his phone.

It was a two-and-a-half-hour car ride to the orchard. John, his sister and I all crammed in the backseat of his dad's sports car with their two poorly trained slobbering cockapoo-doodles. The clawed Oodles pawed at our bare legs, drooling in our laps, while in the front seat his parents squawked about theoretical wrong turns that they blamed one another for taking in the future. Once there, the dogs got left in the hot car. The family decided that, instead of walking we take the tractor ride across the orchard. I boarded the plank with the fat and the lazy, jealously watching from in between the red metal bars of the cargo cage as the young and limber frolicked through the orchard, biblically holding hands, giggling through the grassy aisles under the canopies of bowed branches, heavy with ripe fruit.

Our crowd of fleshy bodies off-loaded, families peeled off, each unit claiming a nearby tree, just as we did. I wish I could describe our tree as being something; small, sulking and unimpressive maybe; large sprawling and littered with strange yellow birds, perhaps, but the tree we chose was none of those things. It was indistinguishable from the others in the orchard, cast in a glaringly average amount of light, bearing a reasonable amount of decent enough fruit. No one wanted to pick apples. No one liked apples. "It doesn't make sense to pick the apples and pay for them if we're not gunna eat them," advised his father, forever the wise businessman, while his sister fixed her hair in her phone. I've gone paleo so I can't eat fruit anyway," John voiced proudly for the fifth time since breakfast, prancing around the field in his new Nikes like a chubby old goat that thought it was a kid. Beside our insignificant tree, we assembled into the stock photo for family fun, made the moment we had journeyed there to make for the refrigerator.

In the end, they all got donuts and ate them in the car. Even John-gone-paleo was eating donuts, three, in fact, his crumby arms guarding the cakey O's from the tongues of the uncontrollable cockoodles. When a cockoodle is trapped in a car with people eating donuts their eyes go real buggy, and the four eyes in the backseat looked like I felt, like they were under so much pressure they were about to bleed.

Back in the present, behind a glass door, a row of peach diet Snapples are sweating.

"She was saying we looked so happy," the voice of the same boy from the back seat says to me now in the bodega, though he's hardly the same as the boy in the backseat, he's more like an expired idea.

"Oh John!" Kazmir says, as he Ping-pongs his head back and forth between John and my body, emphasizing how bizarre it is to see us standing here next to one another, as if neither of us has already felt the strangeness. Kaz holds my hot sandwich hostage in his hands.

Kazmir, I remember, knows in excruciating detail why John and I aren't talking anymore, somewhat embarrassing. John and I may have had a loud fight next to the chip aisle on more than one occasion, where some words were screamed about the women. There may have been a night in December when I threw John's phone on the bodega floor, stomped on it with my lace-up boots and then grabbed a container of liquid detergent and emptied the slow falling slime onto the device while screaming *Satanic saggy-balled mama's boy small turtle-mouthed craigslist panty licking bitch.* Or something to that effect. I feel the same urgency now, I realize—the urgency to obey the exit sign. Kaz throws John a smile, says to him "It's you!" Kazmir's you is the best kind, it's clean and genuine with no hint of frustration or longing.

The two of them jump into a fast-paced conversation about this first-person shooter game they both play. I make horrified laser beam eyes at Kazmir, communicating that I don't appreciate his friendly enthusiasm towards John. Kazmir is on my team and even if they both spend their free time shooting civilians on the same platform, I am the real-world thing they have in common, literally their fucking origin is: me. Plus, this is my neighborhood. I do not play or care about their stupid game, and I am a decent enough person to deserve loyalty from somewhere, at the very least from my bodega guy. Isn't he the one who thinks that the only thing that should matter in a country is love? And please, for love itself, my egg and cheese.

They are yapping away about command combinations, unlisted codes that enable certain weapon boosts, until it finally looks like Kazmir is about to pause and do what is right and hand me my sandwich. "But that button combo never works for me, even when I hold the trigger ... are you sure you don't have to XXABY?" John familiarly whines, and Kaz is so enchanted by his whine that he forgets to do what is right and instead puts my egg and cheese on the counter top, resting his latexed paw on it like a guard. Kaz confirms that the code only works after you've stepped on the little green box in the hallway that transports you to the bazaar.

"Yeah, cool, yeah, I think ...yeah, cool! ...cool, yeah!" John says like he's starting to get it, though I suspect only loosely. He isn't the kind of guy who likes to admit when he doesn't understand.

From what I can gather about this universe I am excluded from, here's how it works: a CGI boot steps on the box and, for a limited time only, one's avatar gets highlighted by something they call 'the green glow.' A novice doesn't think twice about his glow, for the average player it just looks glowy and they think "huh?" A player adapts to the green aura, instead focusing on the immediate pressure to shoot at incoming bodies. When one has the green glow they're actually operating in an alternate level, chasing bad guys through an identical landscape, shooting bullets down the hallways of a same-seeming world that's actually a duplicate. If the glow wears off before you've successfully thumbed the combination, well then you've blown it. Time is up. Kaz thinks that John tends to blow it when he gets the glow which is, knowing John, quite likely. At random, other misunderstood totems will appear, yes, there are new empty levels waiting to get unlocked, infinite codes and possibilities that lead to total domination, but this new special level which is the level that the two of them are still fucking talking about is the best new level either of them has gotten to as of yet, and compared to the older-new levels they've made it to before it is a much bigger accomplishment for a variety of mundane reasons which from what I can tell are: 1) the scenery 2) weapon power boosters 3) moments of temporary night vision.

I eyeball my sandwich knowing that once it is in my hands I will be emancipated. I think towards the future, how good it will feel to be released from this, free, outside, inhaling the exhaust of 14th street, dodging the underpaid bicycle delivery guys who illegally circumnavigate traffic laws while they artfully avoid spilling oily lo mein from their nylon sacks. Kazmir looks back-and-forth between John and me watching us like we're live television, with the slightest potential to be somewhat entertaining when it happens. Kaz hands me the sandwich. I cradle the paper bundle in my hands, like it's a warm precious baby that hasn't been aborted. It smells like salt pepper and butter. Kazmir is giving me one of his looks, that annoyingly familiar look of I-know-something-you-don't-know when I see my other dead ex-boyfriend's reflection in the glass refrigerator door that imprisons the Sprite. My chipped manicure clings to the dying warmth of my freedom. Once again, the skin. The body. The face. The "man." The overhead fluorescents click like they sometimes do, the yellow greening.

This is not a grocery store, it's just the bodega and because of this unfortunate glitch in the scenery my two dead ex-boyfriends think it's okay to walk right up to each other. "G— god," I say it quietly but with my whole voice. The men don't even notice the light, but I am not a man and I know this light, its rules, its thick green glue, binding my feet to the linoleum.

"Nice to meet you," John says to John genuinely. I can't believe John said hi to John before he said hi to me except that I can believe it because if there is one thing I've observed about reality it's that reality gets off on being unbelievable. Plus, if there is anything I've learned from history, it's that being done with me is a real thing that people love to bond over. "Nice to meet you too," John says right back to the John I loved first. It isn't only their names, or the looks of amusement on the Johns faces. They look the same as one another, something I've intentionally never thought about. Through the greenish light the stunned John's see their own uncanny resemblance, each face wears a look of awe in seeing itself so clearly plastered on the skull of another John. I fantasize exit strategies. I envision the many worlds that don't make space for the people who I am done with, alternate landscapes complete with mazes of gigantic yellow water slides, margaritas, a population completely comprised of beautiful strangers. I'll pay Kaz next time, I think. I'll army crawl along the ledge of wintergreen packets.

Each John studies a John with the intensity of a child in a mirror, trying to memorize its own face. John's forehead is slightly broader, I think, whereas John's eyes are a teensy bit closer together, but I can't tell if this minute distinction is accurate or if it's just illusory lighting. "Wow," John says, looking right into Johns eyes, the same eyes that once told me he would till death do us part if I adopted this puppy we'd seen eating scraps of shredded paper in a 10 storefront window on Sixth avenue. "I've heard rumors that she has a type but I never thought—wow."

"Wow is— wow," John responds. They each hold the shapes of their mouths a little too long after they make the w shape, like a turned off fountain of twin statues blowing invisible whistles, stunned demonic cherubs.

"I hear somebody's got an art show in November," John says. I feel like a doll, a body of parts waiting to be moved by a girl. I am the girl, I say to myself, this is my body, but it will not let itself be moved by me. I shake my head as if this is something that happened yesterday and I'm reviewing todays disaster with Kazmir after the fact, once the bodega has become a safe space again, once the natural florescence, if you can call it natural, has returned. Tomorrow the sandwich I'm about to eat will only be as relevant as every other sandwich I've consumed in my past; my hunger will be fresh; I will only have new fried eggs to look forward to. Tomorrow, I will appreciate eggs on a whole new level.

"I saw somebody's got an art show in November," John says again. The some- body he's referring to is the person in my body, the somebody is me. I nod yes, even though it's just a group show, technically not confirmed as of yet. He puts his hand on my shoulder lightly, trying to exude warmth, like a child on the spectrum who's been trained to connect. I think of the upcoming show, it's a relief to think to a time other than the time that is now here, any place other than this place, to the abandoned battlefield on my apartment floor where piles of unfinished drawings collect dust. I'll be showing some of my crude-looking character landscapes, done in pencil and crayons—cerulean stick-figures commuting on a lazy horizon line, apricot ladies in strappy platforms walking their cobalt husbands on leashes down Madison avenues, a single sepia figure vomiting on the train tracks below Canal. I have twenty different mulberry women pushing black strollers into crowded grocery stores at rush hour, a self-portrait of a circle crying pee out her window onto the roof of a taxi. Many of the figures are linked to thought bubbles that are empty, looming crowds pregnant with potential, turning my little guys into sadder versions of themselves, like they're just haphazard blueprints for a cartoon still waiting for its writer. Like me now, versions of little characters trapped in iterations of pause. What the hell am I going to wear to this opening anyway? The pink suede pumps that chafe the heels? The Dries Van Noten pointy-toed patent thigh highs that leave me knockkneed the morning after? I should pick up some condoms, just in case. I know I should finish the work before I fixate on the look. The work is what should matter, though shoes linger in the front of my mind, tempting my feet with possibility. By the time I allow myself to reenter my bodega, I see that time hasn't actually stopped and I've missed the conversation. Kazmir and my two ex-John's probably imagine that I've been staring blankly at the tower of toilet paper stashed above the racks of Lysol wipes. Or, as it appears, none of them are at all preoccupied with my ambient toilet paper focus, conversation is moving quite nicely without me.

Luckily, this John has also started to play the same computer game that John and Kaz have been talking about.

"Aren't you just in love with it?!" John asks, excited to be together with a group of men who all play the same game alone. John goes on to explain how, the guns, at first, made him uncomfortable, but now he's so into the game, it's even better than something called "spank bang." Everybody but me seems to be familiar with the spank bang. Can't say I'm surprised to hear that John's come around to the guns. This makes sense for his personality. He's one of those guys who posts feminist anti-violence free-gender blah blah jargon on his feed, lately a slew of articles about female body positivity. Which do make me wonder, now that I'm here in this stuck body, if you're no longer positive you have a body does that mean you're not body positive? Anyway, as someone who knows him intimately, I know that the only reason he's so vocal about "women's rights" is because all he secretly wants is to be able to choke the hell out of one. This was one of my favorite things about fucking John, the reason John and I were good together. He was a real hook. The real deal. Once upon a time, I selected John because he was the kind of guy who cried when a dog got shot in a movie (a wiggly thing), but since then, I've viewed his computer history (barb).

The three of them moronically start humming what I assume must be its theme song, which has an appropriately intense melody, a cross between Star Wars and the first movement of Beethoven's fifth symphony. *Talk about a song that makes you want to kill yourself*, I try to ESP this message to Kaz, who's smiling at me creepily through his humming. Kaz doesn't get the memo or miss a note. Songs like this were literally written to go on forever until you die. It goes on so long my legs get somehow even heavier. I wonder if I should squat to wait it out, but decide against it.

We were just talking about that glow ...do you know about it?" John asks John, who doesn't but says he's been having some curious thoughts every time he gets green and then transports to the bazaar. His "curious thoughts" are teenage in complexity, mostly comprised of um's. So, tedious, he leaves me with no choice. I squat down, and when I do Um John barely looks at me, says in his pitying voice, "What are you waiting for?" nodding at my sandwich baby, now cold in my hands. "She'll never stop squatting in public," John says to John and they both laugh like a pair of tight-ham-stringed lunatics.

Much better off at this new level, I resort myself to silence as they refocus on their shared world, a world that matters more than any world I could ever be in. "It seems pretty clear that something is happening BTS," John says to John, who nods rigorously in agreement. "What is BTS?" asks Kaz, and a John explains to him that it means, um, behind the scenes. "There are these commands that ..." "I only figured it out because ..." "Are you sure that's the right combination?" "WAIT! I made it there once!" my old best friend says with a particular assuredness that gives me no choice other than to remember him as someone I once really knew. We are all so quiet, it's as if the bodega has been swept under by a damp magic, the buzz of the fluorescents tremble the glass refrigerator doors. "Whaaaa—what happened?" John asks, and a miraculously um-less John starts to speak clearly and slowly, like this is a story he's telling from the future, as if he is a grandfather, aged out of the mortal responsibility to be respectful of everyone else's time. The griddles gone dry and smells like the smell of something unburnable burning, like iron, maybe steel. "When you manipulate that green ...I guess you're calling it the glow ...things don't reverse they ...they ...
" The bodega light flickers. I rest my elbows on the ledges of my knees and hold the sandwich in both hands like it's some kind of offering. I look down at my feet.

"That's so beautiful, incredible." John says to John and John nods and I wonder what has just happened here? I silently shame myself for dropping out of such an important scene. The three of them are looking at one another in a way that suggests they all know something I don't. I'm worried that the thing they all know so much about, this thing they all seem to understand that I can't, is something other than the game, something other than the glow, like maybe it's me. Even though this is my bodega, my breakfast, and Kaz is mine, the bodega seems pregnant with the belief that I'm the one who's not supposed to be here.

Kazmir looks fully engaged inside his apron, triangulating his eyes between our three bodies in the space unfazed by my squatting. "Oh John!" Kazmir says solemnly, "You have really given me something to think about. It is like what it says in the great book, the believer is like a mirror to other believers."

They are all so quiet it's like they're praying, before Kaz breaks the sacrament with one of his winks. "The Usuals?" Kaz asks the two John's who both nod hungry yesses. When Kaz says "the usuals," a painful heat erupts in my belly, like that time I accidentally drank turpentine in Mexico.

The burn of betrayal that accompanies the word *usual* as it comes out of Kaz's mouth wipes their green glowing world away, and I am overcome with a certain feeling that I hate but don't have a name for. I remember a time I thought I'd forgotten, when my father came to my art open house in elementary school and had picked up a drawing of the ocean that a boy with my same initials had drawn with crayons, and (thinking it was mine), began praising me about how good my work was getting, what an amazing improvement this seascape was compared to what he'd seen in my earlier drawings. The ocean had these dumb smiling swans around it. It was blue and the swans were yellow in the immature sunlight. After that open house, I'd gone home and looked at my art. It was probably just for a minute but I was seven so give me a break. I looked at my art for a long, long time. Mine had been an illustration of the car crash that my dad and I had shared only a few weeks before; broken glass sprinkled around a roadkill raccoon, the emerald green car plunged into a brick wall as the horizon line framed an approaching ambulance. In reality, the crash had been fantastic, there was a dramatic swerve and there was snow that swirled up on the windshield as we pushed through it and the moment after we'd both snapped back into consciousness after slamming into the brick wall I'd looked up at him and his expression mirrored mine with a dumbfounded beauty that can only be attributed to unspoken feelings of great relief when you mutually rediscover that you are both still alive. We were equally present in that moment, checking that the other's limbs were intact before knowing if our own bones were still in place, energized by the shards of glass that stuck to our necks and our parkas, our silhouettes reflecting light as we burst out through the car doors and wobbled out into the clean, bright dust of the snow. When I looked at the drawing afterwards, it was clear that this piece was unmistakably mine. It was my story, our story, or so I thought. One could observe my prehensile grip in the shaky lines of Crayola, and the entire color palette clashed with itself in a way that few children ever perceive as being a good-looking combination. He wanted me to be the kind of kid, like blimpy Leon Delver, who painted happy swans on top of oceans where they don't even live. In a group of unexceptional children my dad could, and would still choose the wrong child. I decided then that I wasn't intended to be his. It dawned on me that all predetermined familial assignments and the loyalties that came along with them had been arranged at random. I might have not known how to say it in the way I've just said it but I felt it completely, in the way someone can only feel something completely when they can't access the language to talk about it yet.

"I haven't seen you around in a bit." Kaz says to John while he toasts their two rolls, before he asks "How's Nancy?" Nancy? I unscrew the top of my coconut water and take a swig, channeling the powers of the orphaned monkey slaves. I absorb their abandonment, their anger, and in just a few gulps my primate parts have been snapped back into the bones of my body. Electrolytes. The bodega clicks, the greenish light drops out, is replaced by the usual urinary yellow. Using what exists of my core, I rise from my squat.

"WHO IS NANCY?" says my voice. I guess, she's back and it sounds like she's horrified and really not appreciating that a story where I am supposed to be the center has not only given itself permission to revive and unite our supposed to be dead ex-dudes, but is now casually introducing a character that I don't and shouldn't need to know about, worst of all this character is a woman who's been with John enough times to have a name. "What is this?" she says again out loud. "Is breakfast some kind of joke?" Even if she has to have a name why does Kazmir have to know it and even if he does know it why does he have to say it so enthusiastically? He is on my team.

I scroll through my girlodex for shadows of Nancys from social media. I'm having trouble deciding if Nancy works in PR for Banana Republic or if she is a pube-less stripper at that crusty Bushwick strip club where all the girls have armpit hair and MA's in gender studies. Kaz knows he shouldn't have said Nancy as soon as he says the name, and not so smoothly transitions to weather, the most boring subject of all eternity, and while the three of them are happily debating tomorrow's forecast, I ponder the possibilities of Nancy. Whether she is wearing a polo or reclaimed pasties, I'm sure she is younger than I am. Looking down at the breakfast bundle in my hands, I think about how unlikely it is that Nancy would eat something like this roll. She couldn't do gluten, even on vacation, not with a body like that.

"This is entirely strange," the undead say to each other. "Do you live near here? Is this your bodega?" says the John who once kissed my forehead and sang me to sleep asks the John who once made me a mobile of dangling action figures which he hung over my bed to protect me. I get a churning hit of nausea, or is that tenderness? The John's talk about how neither of them live nearby, they still both live off the G, which I assume means that they are either stalkers or fucking Nancies that live in my neighborhood. It isn't a coincidence that the John who once secretly filmed me sucking him off and the John who once stole my change jar to get a pack of Newports both lived off of the most inconvenient, unreliable train; that's symbolic synchronicity. He promised he deleted the video, through boyish tears, but who knows what still exists on the hard drive. He smoked the whole pack and didn't save me one cigarette. In my world, sometimes the fate of your own mouth gets taken out of your own hands. The John who loves his mother tells the John who has no mother that it's so nice to finally meet him and touches his arm affectionately. They exchange screen names and agree to be in touch about the glow. I imagine them reuniting on another platform, touching guns.

"G—god," I say to no one in particular. "God," I say again, but this time, I'm thinking about anything but hard drives, anything but the Johns, I'm thinking about the G train. How the G always stops in the middle of the tracks. Kazmir flips green bell peppers for their usuals.

The vegetable reminds me that they both have bad taste in breakfast. I know that all the men at my bodega know exactly how I feel about green peppers, and I know that at least one of them will get gassy from the peppers within the hour, but looking back and forth between them, I don't care to remember which one has the more sensitive digestion.

# Rachel Levitsky

## Against Travel

*FOR DANA*

I dream en route from St. Petersburg, Mississippi to St. Louis, Florida. My vampire lovers are precariously situated in a novel by James Hannaham. More numbers of us are vampires than originally thought. All of us. You can tell by the loose and missing skin of our teeth. Our outfits were cut out skimpily in Vs so skimpy the queen who could fly flew away. From all of it. Maybe I am she. They say I am. I want to say I told you so to one of you, in particular. What good does foresight do and who needs it when you are like me, queen vampire who can but doesn't always fly away. Yeah, sometimes I stay. I earn a mouthful and keep it to myself. As I am. As they say I am.

## *Against Travel*

FOR TOPHER

I wake, without reason. The television fog meets with fog on the street. No one need be judged, ever again. Harshly or on the brow of what possibly. If I open the papers first thing in the morning what becomes of my dream. If I don't think of you what becomes me. I offered five skinny women ten pounds each. I was rejected from a hot bathroom encounter by one who wouldn't pass their or her or his ethics. If we are saying too much, as I suspect we are, what becomes the occupation. Writer. Writing. Saying take the money...it's a medium. I think three things about the two of them. One by one shake them off. The things I think, not the two of them.

## Against Travel

*FOR MONA AND DONALD (2)*

Mona says bone broth. Taylor sees lemon water and a bath. Dr Steve agrees. There
will be blood. Or according to the practice, there should be. The problem here, says
K. I tried wanting to be happy. Mona and Donald come from a similar age, way
of practice. I read the newspaper to find out just how bad really. The stock market
climbs then climbs again. The banks take time. It's on their side, and oh, his. This is
not a pessimistic poem. No rental offers come for Mona and Donald. No level place
for them to stand.

Newspapers debate what he knew and knows. Foucault says maybe he knows and
maybe he thinks he knows. Suzanne says we have to be willing to give things up. I
picture it. Up comes what white people, and I am one, said or grunted. Some fear,
something crude about the homeless and their city shelter. That it's dark at night. Tri-
ple pay three blocks away. Mona and Donald have two months left until their storied
old school becomes history and dust. Only magic not probability on their side. Mini
electronic placards say, Someone Out There Loves You. And, it's white people's job to
smash white supremacy. It's a white knuckle it kind of job.

## *Against Travel*

*FOR RUTH*

Between the course and the course its precipitation transmogrifies from snow mist to snow to hail to snow to mist to rain. Along the same river and about it a big ancestral feeling as if for a change something Good has happened in the zone of memory usually reserved for that which keeps us staring at the window not there. No concrete fill. No reconstruction of some eternal shiny city of anyone's dream. It's just a shitty interior wall. Now it's the river that's changed and no more feeling. It's not yet connected, by tributary or tribute, just some vague similarities of sound and umlaut. Is an umlaut an accent or a diacritical mark. Anyway, it's pretty here just the same. In the distance we see the castles we've seen somewhere before.

## SUZI GARCIA

*Dorothy—*

Together we can rewrite that day they took you, faster than any twister
    we've seen.

Kansas grass and four walls that are more alive
than us, but it's the perfect background for a #selfie,
chola transplant, dark lipstick & slicked back hair.

We are in the midst of a prairie, Dorothy, and this is almost a simple
    moment except it's not—

Suddenly, that is no sky, this ceiling. Look around,
we're in a corner, one of four. Look—we are another generation, and today
I feel we cannot change
a goddamn thing. Against the wall,
put a bed, the kind that closes on top.

## Escape Is Possible If You Just Fucking Stand Still

Don't you try to talk to me          about wild moons, about how big it was when we
left the house and how we are chasing it but it gets smaller and once I lose it behind
the clouds,          the light will be completely gone.          Don't even fucking
say the words *next time I swear.*  So what

  if a stopping place is unknown?  We'll make it this time, I swear. I'm sure there are
vital clues hidden in music if I can get some damn reception. Worst case scenario:
hit a tree, watch the car burn, read smoke signals to find a new map.

                    The feathers on my hat droop;          I can't see.

Let's go home. No, let's not.          Let's stop here, build a home out of the sheets in
our backseat. Our cats will keep us warm.


Use a lit cigarette to etch
new doctrines on the sides of brass goblets. Bury it
in the earth          (*preciosa*)
                    will it grow? Focus,
                    there is room for error, but only
                    if your art is intricate enough.  Make sure
                    the bridge is there too, even if we can't find it now.
                    And when you carve me, fix the feathers, ok?

                    They should stand tall, they should stretch beyond the rim,
hide my face

                    in flowers. And you know what else should be there?
                    Birds.  Engrave life, because I think we can create
                    imminence. The seasons will change— I've been promised—
but until then,

gather broken boxes,          set them on fire, let's see what comes of ashes.
Fuck, who knows? Maybe a poem will appear.

# Ariana Reines

## Report

Without headphones without
Book. At once muscular
And carbuncular & wearing
A dress that could only
Be called Hulk Hogan I went
To the meeting. Because
I had to. Because not to
Could have only been called
Maladaptive. Well what kind
Of poet were you the people
In power demanded to know
In so many worlds. An around-
The-world poet I guess. Two
Fresh pink boys had moved
Down the block. I'd
Seen them in their college
Sweatshirts on my way
To the train, wearing the rubbery
Haunted look of sheltered
Youths before whose eyes
Many decapitations and porns
And little else of moment
Had passed. Much to await
From such bright youth

## Wasting Away in This Vanilla Darkness

for CA Conrad

Kegel now before the monarchs
Flutter up under the lamps to smoke
The guard coming toward us
Looks like Felix Morisseau-Leroy
Hurry the rest of them won't be beautiful
Like him. Metallic taste of old
Cherry Coke. These are the mechanic's keys
Don't move them. It happened
To be a moment I was feeling bad
About myself. We were in the souvenir
Kiosk behind the throne room
The arrow in my compass began
To quiver, solemn colonels slicing key
Limes into keys into a tureen of wastoid
Pukes lightly slapped with a plateletty
Lasagne by the white hand of a handsome
Waiter in a battalion of balls
On a billiard table loaded w eternally
Tween thoughts reconstellating
The diamond sense of genocide's very
Worst ideas. It was like a portrait
Of happy people that you and I have
Certainly both seen. I was only
Trying to recover a sense of myself
I am not trying to be forgiven
For that I am just telling you
Strange bran steaming up from my genitals
Gems are the eyes of god said Julian and so
Is everything else we added. And how did birds
Begin? **VOID IF DETACHED**
I came upon the ruins of a bird in a beet
Field in Normandy. I gathered them
Up & carried them quietly into Lithuania
I went into Lithuania very very quietly

& silently sleep stopped coming
Some of my family had escaped
About a hundred years earlier. I might
Have been the first to return. I hid
Everything I could recollect and also
What I could not behind my books
And I hid it behind my clothing and hair
Snowden was somewhere in the Moscow
Airport the day at Duty Free a Russian
Woman mistook me for a star. I'm
Not anybody famous I told her. She
Did not want to believe. The forests
Looked like a big black boar
Capital had a different way of flowing
It seemed iridescently to mean a new
Virulent strain of heterosexuality
A lot of striptease bars, Zaras & sex
Clubs, shining black caviar, lurid orange roe
The rainbow spread across the surface of whatever
Spilled. It shone on the mallard's neck. And all over the crow.

# Queens

First part of the wicker of un-understanding
Ne plus ultra of asshole boyfriends
Who was trying to pull my arm
I fell heavily to sleep with jellyfish
In my stomach, there had already
Been a curious headache of nuts, deep
Decay of death & unholiness, then a high
Neighbor speakerphoning with a woman
All night. He goes **BRRRRRRRP** and
**DRRRRRRRRRRRRT** with his mouth
When he is aroused. You know why I like you
He speakerphones on the stair. You
Notice every little thing about me.
Then in the night my friend across
The hall cried out **MY FRIEND**
**IS DEAD** & there was a commotion
& the matriarch downstairs shouted
Her men back into the house screaming
**I'M LOCKING THE DOOR, THE COPS**
**ARE COMING.** Then police and paramedics
Filled the building and their whirling red lights.
They carried the neighbor down in a chair.
I heard him talking so he wasn't dead
In bed now in a stocking cap and a button-
Down shirt. **CHEESEBURGER**
**IN PARADISE** it says. We wanted to be close
To each other. I wanted to feel people
Living. I wanted to live too. The gate
On the building slamming closed
I tell myself I'm sitting here unmolested
Then I remember the night J got arrested
After a bird chirped between movements
Of Mozart's Mass in C

## Ramayana

*for Carol Rama (1918–2015)*

Here is where I first stood transparent

To my mind.  You must have seen me

But I can't tell you when it began

When my friend was opening her bluefish

Laying lemons all along his chilled raspberry

Flesh. Not then. But here

Like a foretaste of dental rot

I nearly caught an eel once

He tied himself in knots

Frightening away all the fish

The penny in my little pussy convulsed in horror

When I know

What I know

That's not a shadow in your kitchen

It is a bug shimmering

Look at him waving his rays

Inside you tickling all you don't

Want to know that you know

This shoe I drag survivalistically

Beneath the tarted perambulator

In which by God I have seated my soul

To get fucked by this shoe

By the mistress whose walk is a shoe-limping fuck

By the mistress whose limp is a bone-fucking bed

Whose past is a braid

Whose first is a maid

Whose last are tongues

Of flame strawberry slabs

Salivating up the ass of the bear

I crown myself with this diadem

Spunk and wool

Osso bucco

You are alive in Turino

There I go kneeling

Supplicant to the years here I go

Knighting myself in my tits

In zits like iron ball bearings

In ball-and-chains ballasting

Us to the beginning

Of the end of this world

THIS POEM WAS ORIGINALLY COMMISSIONED BY PAUL B. PRECIADO FOR AN EXHIBITION IN BARCELONA CALLED THE PASSION ACCORDING TO CAROL RAMA, WHILE THE ARTIST WAS STILL ALIVE.

# CHRISTOPHER PATRICK MILLER

## Bridget Bishop

In my own way, haven't I proven it?
If someone had asked me. If I could know
Villagers. Like your dream,
I would have disemboweled your children
With silver talon, limped the shadows of furniture
Across your wounds. I would have sold all my stock
And eaten kelp, growing forests in my stomach.
Tell me, when life is furiously short and death is a crawl
Do you listen for me in your broken phone?
Do you not talk over me when I start singing in snow?
It is not a dream, you are really surprised
I shot everyone in the car wash
Then went on to the school
But isn't this what you said I was capable of
Putting on the cloak you deem invisible
By becoming the shape you wanted to see
Coming home, proffering my darker organs
The word for this is mutual aid. A legislative compromise
Balanced on the old growth of toes, I
Would have danced. I would have closed an argument
About paying the national family bills
Congressmen reminding us that we all
Have to balance our budgets whose
Remainder is interest, interests
The strangely confident foundation of our right
And families show their love
By setting you out on your own with strong teeth
Salt in the back street, what a recession
What is everything I would have done and continue to do
With a satisfied mind it is written in the books
You read. My life for you is over,
Dragging away in bed sheets your doubtful appliances
Blame not the cows who follow me into the sea

## Strangers Globing in a Village

No mountain cross to mistake
Worth his weight
When he leaned down to kiss the dirt
On the man's bailing legs
Rounding the fatal blood weather
Killers killing you for the killing
What kind of ruin is that
When the life that surfaces is not your own
Bone geodes that walk and catch up our migrant skin
Blue flowing hounds in and out of plastic brooms
Keening hairs as they pass, old friends
With souls never distracted, vocables
Tensing among hieroglyphs, my love
Did you know how low we could go, how long
We could hold love there.  No snow
At the pass, partners in cruelties
We could never even imagine
Did you know how easy it had become
To rhyme home with roam?  I never know
Until I say it.  I couldn't follow
How hard the earth
Is packed for us, country dust caked in your mouth
A conversation we could never have
Potholes in our lawns.  Gravel
Craven weeds, parking lots split up into courts
Of public opinion.  Don't listen to the white-
Haired man explaining the value form
Extended himself into a pride before a young crowd
Every action a dream of a conceit
Before saying sorry

A split, we get evicted, or despite of
These horribly ornate excavations
About gifts and obligations to others, compensatory
Blooms for the terrible liabilities of flesh, really

Lost my head there, like a deflated father
Would tell his son
Every pigeon eats the next one
Then becomes a dove
Survival is a tautology
An efficient lie
Of getting on and getting gone
Washed with earned peacefulness, call it systematic meaning
That which exists through itself, fervent scenes of legal notes
About them, by them, for them, and near them
Then a vacuum cleaning towers
Coal modernized as constant light
We assent to carry each other through years of minor
Complaints folding serious cuts
Into our clothes so we can finally sit around a table
Have a conversation

Afford I cannot to understand slowly stuttering
My faults hazarding bullets
Flown into a congregation, only the doors
Burn now but the flames advance, moving into filled land
Rocks bounce on her roof but she is far underground
Her breath snaps blood as blue as radio shine breaking down pieces of man
Eating from the state is not the same as living through it
I can't be anything but this hate, this poor lightning
Flashing through our bitter sleep
The majesty of being human these days
Born out in wheelless cars
Carried by teenage pallbearers
Force your noise
Through kingdoms of windows
I don't want to be anything
But what I heard you say

Why get dressed up in your blues,
Why forever, why the hook
Through John's voice, freezing his works
In a summer of hate, don't stand
Don't lie, pain is a crawl

Living around a neck, the difficulty of just being
Sally Mae, blade of a moan
There is no such thing as a casual mythology
Joe blow crows kissing you last
With nursed revolvers, plenty of white reminders
While glaciers go the way of industrious ghosts
Krill boils and nowhere bees flit to colors
Stinging our stomachs so terribly
Kin felt, cuts on the belly of feet
Who can afford these wistful disguises
I move around incessantly
Trying to be paid, played, delayed in pedals
I go with the ancient organ melodies
Because they are insufficient
More than anger
Or agreement
I am not angry with you.  Look
You have got me in your hands

Full of tomorrow's sugars
I talk like a child of many years
I fill with shadows
Falling in love with each other
These shadows
Not meant for me
Not a hidden alphabet
For us to relish while walking with mealy years
I am not who I think I am
Grain me a character that is given
I will not tell you where we are going
Learning how to ask, as if asking for you
Was a step toward what is where

Paying someone else to tell us
Speech is free for those
Who have already been seen
And heard.  Justice
Destroy it
Before it can work, as much as I try

These languages—crossing my heart
Blue sticks, falling down summer hale
Denting my heart, doing the trouble—
You are right, my heart
Is a tongue that hurts, a keyhole in our gore
James, the alps are stark, plates broke
In the violent conveniences we call dark
Where so many strangers go globing
In abandoned blocks, still wild caves
Truculent through cities, money the truth
In which we say it is and it is not
A world is owed but not this world
It is your turn to parse the poisons in the people we call
He didn't mean it that way
I am a poison
And not just because the world is poisonous
And we have been trained
To name its poisons

You, casual in the right gone crystal of an afternoon
Hear that woman carving into her sleep
The trees splitting skin into bodies, pins through oak
The silhouettes they mingle
Hearing languages never meant for me
Working our heaviness together
One is always working, and not just in these naked times
When you or I can write a world tired
Some hollows of us
Some trumped up booze
If those revenues don't get me
No money will I lose
You'll see me when your sleeping
Doom is a mood
Glass is an impasse, she says,
So I am going in through the window

## Mound Builders

How will we get through these sweet junked middle yards
Leave our soft slaughter work behind
In stains from homes, on

Our clothes, rains in our ears
From the rhythms
We curve while cold walking

Looking in to the crystal hot restaurants
Where everyone eats noodles at once
Where no one shoes

The bottom
Of america
The bottoms a nobody-knows-you river

Flooding your heart, a lost race
Doing that going home slide, expectant, holiday ripe
Not even surprised by so many auctions

In a muddy neighborhood, where abandoned
Falls short of our apotropaic infants
Born without esophagi and me

Screaming, watch this confluence
Move, my how-could-you-build-such-things-walk
From the top of this medieval mound

Where I show off the unreal crop in my teeth, ancient real
Like the reverberations you hear, picking my bones
In cavities of a caved city rumored by money

Flintknapped, kidnapped, what ransom will you pay
Commodity Monks, Priests of Revitalization
If I feed you the places

You look out from. Feel me
In every basket of dirt you carry up at night
To pour and balance your scales

# BLAKE BUTLER

## The Approaching Planet

*PUNDIT*: What do you recall about the darkness?
*THE OLDEST LIVING ASTRONAUT*: Absolutely everything.

Between commercials for brain insurance, the only major news channel still remaining reports the discovery of a significant new planet: one, they say, that on its surface looks exactly like our own. It seems ridiculous at first, seeing photos so much like those we have come to know as Earth presented onscreen as somewhere else, somewhere unknown, and alongside infographics that explain its present distance of hundreds of millions of light years away from where we are; and yet the longer that we look and listen, absorbing the information, we can't help but grow concerned. As though the planet appears to be exactly like ours, visually *a perfect copy*, so it appears, average surface temperatures on the twin are estimated at an average of just under 200 degrees F. Furthermore, in zooming down to surface level through animated cells accessed onscreen, though we do find certain remaining manmade structures—lengths of scaffolding organized around large pale windowless cubes; long strips of railways devoid of markings, exits; remainders of cities that resemble ours but never quite the same in their design—no life has as yet been recognized, the pundits report. It is like our Earth, but remodeled, and then evacuated, or exterminated, at least so far as we can tell.

More important than its matching image, they inform us, is the path and rate of the twin planet's present approach. It is aimed directly at us, by all most scientific of accounts, moving at an unprecedented speed for what an object of its size should yet be able. The planet has, since first becoming known less than a month prior in only our most protected sectors, traversed nearly a third of the distance remaining between us and it, continuing to gain ground by the hour, showing no intent of wavering. Within weeks it will be visible to the naked eye, and not long after, barring an adjustment in its approach, it will pass our planet at a distance closer than halfway to where the moon was believed once to have been, right through all that empty space we'd been trying for so long to pass the laws allowing advertising to command, said stalemate about which has nothing at all to do with anything.

*But so there is no need right now to panic,* the anchors submit, bearing the same flattened expressions by which they'd told us of the War for Empty Space, of the outbreaks of immediate aphasia among survivors, of the patterns of disappearance and reappearance of major landmarks. We have come to rely on their poise amid these times, their refusal to overreact, the plastering feeling of how their voices set onto us, settle in. *And though we know the planet is approaching, we do not anticipate it to wreck into us head-on; we only expect for now it might affect our weather systems, and so our crops, and so our ways of life amid its presence. We do not believe that we will die, only that we will be significantly affected in numerous and unpredictable ways of being, some of which we have already long foreseen, and are preparing in the near future to remedy in equally unprecedented fashion, to the benefit of all.*

*And so the last thing you and your family should be sure to know about the approaching planet,* they continue, *is that no matter how close it grows, how hard any one of us might wish to understand and accept the present science, not all persons will be able to see the planet with their own eyes.* Something about its light, its all too familiar shape and brand of color, based on their testing, allows only, they estimate, one in seven citizens to see and understand that it is there. *Only citizens of exceptional intelligence and keenest sense, they submit, are expected to be able. Do not be alarmed if you are among those who for whatever reason yet cannot; it does not mean you are any less a person than the rest, only that you might require their assistance in application of prevention behaviors as we come together as a nation to deal with this unprecedented threat, which we surely will, because we must, because we have the gift of information.*

Going forward, the following PSAs take over to explain, all citizens are advised and bound by Congress to extend the periods through which we wear our National Masks, which had been previously only required during working hours, throughout all hours, day and night, *mostly because we are not sure yet of what effect the approaching planet's makeup and decorum might have on our atmosphere, our future outlook.* Additionally encouraged are an array of presently non-mandatory products by the makers of Error Gel and X-All-Eyes-Out, ranging from swimsuits that simulate the presence of actual water to peppermint candies known to have mostly pleasant-dream inducing and extra-spiritual effects, all of which each household will be auto-subscribed to in lieu of manually opting out by handwritten statement of hesitancy, some of which you may or will still be billed for and have installed without permission; *as by the time we realize there is something we should fear or prevent, it may be too late,* a grinning model offers through her expensive silver teeth, *it may even be inside us; it may have become us.*

That night again there is no moon. There has not been a moon in at least weeks, nor any other planets, though we can hardly remember other planets, but it is still the absence of the moon that hurts the most; it had been ours. The space remaining where the moon should be seems fuzzed up, buzzing almost, perhaps slightly caving into itself surrounded by all the nothing—as if the thing had become swallowed into a hole right where it stood. Some are still able to persuasively describe the day of the moon's recorded disappearance: how whole crowds of people fainted and frothed in hordes in open air malls across the continent; how our limbs thereafter felt heavier than usual, paler than usual, dizzying to have to lift; how then when days later the sale of snake eggs artificially went up, we all began to eat the eggs for all three meals whether we'd even ever liked eggs of any kind or not, and always in separate rooms, hoarding our intake unto ourselves, wanting to hear the sounds the chewing makes inside our head again, like private music, ours and ours alone; like falling and falling.

+

There are those, within mere hours, despite previously reported estimations, for whom the new planet in open sky is as clear as day. Some calmer folk might mistake it for pending aberrations in the weather, they imagine, a smear on the seeing visors; and yet surely there it is; or so say even certain major figures both of science and of cloth alike, creating immediate ideological disturbances in each field, the loudest among them raising the highest beams. *It is right there,* they cry into the rolling recorders, *and growing larger as we speak. Look out and try again to see what we can see already, ahead of schedule. I mean really try.*

Try as they might, many others less incensed or bound to wish, when told precisely how and where to look and what to see, see absolutely nothing beyond the sky as it had always been in recent years; that is, *so silken and untouchable; so now.* Even new viral photographs of the horizon said to clearly depict the planet stark and bright against the curvature of blank to others evoke only a continuity of empty space, and thereby serve as proof of fact of the idiocy of both the seers and the believers. *It's just a fucking picture of the Earth,* they type into threads of countless forums, *all cut and paste; my kid could do it; my kid, who just like me, shall not believe.*

So there are those who have witnessed the twin planet, and those who want to, and those who believe those who have claimed to are insane. There are those who don't want to hear any more about the twin planet already, tired enough as they are in just trying to continue to get along, to be a person at all during such vicious onslaught as it is to simply stand in daily life. Congressmen and bloggers alike hold their positions, heads of family and youngest toddlers; each are incorporated each in some way into the fold. And so on, and on and on, the flux of information takes its shape, upending boardrooms and homes alike, embroiling each individual person in a would-be shell of their seemingly unique state of belief; who is wrong and who is not wrong; what can be trusted and what is bunk; all of it a silent gore of rampant interruption. As these days no one is an expert. No one believes what anybody says, regardless of position or condition, adhering only exactly ever to who we already are.

By the end of the first week, research shows the factions of those who see the planet outnumber those who do not see it at a ratio of nearly 15:1, a rate quite off from the original prediction, and off too from what seems true by asking around in the streets. It seems much more rare to find a person who believes than who does not in actual barrooms or at parties, despite the precedence of the opinions offered in the media and online. And yet, in time, those who don't see the planet will begin to say they see the planet because they are afraid of the repercussions, and therefore the ratio will rapidly grow more sharp. And regardless of who believes what, what is real will remain real.

+

Amid the fervent state of speculation, prodded by the President, Congress unveils its plan to build the National Ceiling, a project long known to be under works; to protect us; for our protection.

"Despite those who *don't see* what those who *can* claim could destroy us, there remains a constant state of Coming Death," the missive states, "and so it can be agreed at least that more protection is always necessary, that even an unseen enemy can be the most likely to kill. Along these lines, we now officially submit the fact of how the installation of a proper barrier, a shielding ceiling hiding the whole sky, could protect us not only from possible impending rupture but also other sorts of strike we have yet to consider."

The document fails to address how the presence of a National Ceiling would prevent or even limit damage from a possible collision with a planet-sized object, nor does the impending national discussion following the directive somehow ever seem to light for long upon this fact; immediately the conversation turns instead to what supplemental features such a ceiling would enable, as if any debate over whether the construction should actually take place or not has been wiped out from any logic, a black hole of understanding around the cusp of which we can't even realize we aren't addressing.

Within the same day's office hours, an official design is brought to light. Official sponsors champion the concept's undue pulchritude, often stipulated in abstract language rather than in visualization, utilizing dramatized advertisements starred in by athletes, praising the structure's ulterior specs; as in addition to its levels of protection, the ceiling will allow climate control and better weather, not to mention surveillance of public domain on harried streets; and for a change of pace, sometimes, the panels may be used to construct other acts of previously unpredictable magnificence; panes of color clean and old in place of stormy skies; panoramas of historical significance we as a nation cherish, those of all walks; and in general a completely predictable outlook, including scheduled periods for precipitation and of heat, a mechanization of the facets of our atmosphere we've been previously forced to live out at the mercy of, no longer. Every day will be a day worth wandering around in, if not remembering. Every day will be all ours.

The ceiling is voted on unanimously by the national governing officials, who by definition represent the wishes of those who put them where they are in perpetuity.

And so then the conversation turns toward collaboration with the remainder of the the world. Petitions are put out to neighboring countries across the globe requesting their cooperation and their funds. Whatever countries do not commit now will be left out, with no room to spare when the time is nigh. And anyway, it mostly doesn't matter who comes on board with us as long as we are covered. If anything, the non-cooperation of aliens, many of whom are said to claim to not see what we can see, refortifies our passion for our beliefs, whether we believe in them or not, the question of coming impact or effect now not so much a fact as a conclusion already passed, such that soon those who once had claimed to not be able to see the approaching planet now live fully complicated by its needs, can see it up there day and night across the land, as plainly as if there'd never been a time they ever hadn't.

+

Construction of the National Ceiling proceeds apace. *It was already underway from the beginning*, the president announces live on closed circuit tape, *because we knew*; indeed, in some higher valued districts the ceiling is seen to have already appeared, as if by magic, curving up and long over the more paltry constructions, pre-installed to run a nightly background bearing the most beautiful of sunsets, the quickest sunset of all time.

As a people, we first witness the construction of the structure above and around eleven major cities, and from those junctures spreading out in all directions. The work is done at night, by crews of thousands, and thereby along a timeline unprecedented to federal practice. Once installed, the National Ceiling is indistinguishable from prior sky. Even in the midst of being built, sensors in the fibers are designed to reflect the face of atmosphere around it seamlessly, so that we might forget how far the so far partial ceiling actually extends. It is illegal to photograph the process of construction, or to be caught staring too long at the general area of ongoing commotion, by penalty of treason.

Only in our legally enforced sleeping hours can the real work be done, we know, a psychic sort of healing accompanying the application of the translucent panels and beams forming the network hardly hundreds of yards over our heads, under which *the dying cloud within us rises, clusters, forms the skin of the ground of the nameless future*, so says another pundit on TV, whose face appears now against the new night like a moon there watching from above, a complimentary broadcast shown to all in demonstration of the Ceiling's powers, replacing virtual weather, before Full Death Football comes on in its place, helping us to relax again, go loose, feign some small rest before again relinquishing ourselves to the strange rhythm of the masks breathing, so our breathing, in the transition between waking and whatever else there is.

Occasionally, as if for old time's sake, instances of inclement weather will be programmed into the feed, following the old trope that to truly enjoy the greatest times one must remember worse ones, if here now minimized to quiet glow. And otherwise, all there is time for now is beauty, calm.

+

"Time does not exist," a popular, local webcam weatherman reports the morning before his disappearance, still operating among old networks already being forgotten in favor of those who've already updated into the Ceiling's subscription package, already underway. He is one of only hundreds whose face so soon we won't retain, much like our natures. "It is nothing to anyone but god. And god doesn't want to share his ideas. He is silent and only as large as every face knitted together, in one skin. There should be no punctuation in our language. I want a household of the blood I never wasn't."

But time does go on, we know, in claps and packs. Moving from one room to another in the same house might feel like ages passed and bodies shifted, though one can never feel what was once and what still is; where as the words come out of the mouth of any they do not mean what they meant to be said saying and in their reception in the next they are again not the same as what seems to be perceived, as if there are always several hemispheres to the same context in any understanding. One sees anything and cannot correspond it to his or herself, without having appeared along beside it, become touched. It does not matter which part of the storylines you absorb and which you leave to fester on without you.

It is unclear how long the Ceiling's construction in total takes. Unclear also what regions when and where have been affected and to what extent and when, under the measure of the concurrently in-voted Nonawareness Mandate, allowing creation of the location to go unmapped and without protocol for further assessment beyond the eye test, which appears at all points to integrate onto the public with flying colors. And though there are rumors of those who claim the construction of the ceiling is a myth, like the twin planet, and that the difference we see between the new and old sky as the edge of construction passes is in our hearts, or in our minds, these people are also disappeared, or otherwise do not believe their own beliefs really enough to actually believe them, and so remain silent.

As such, the extent of what remains clear or unclear to whom or how to know continues onward unassessed, without regard, as it is generally agreed upon now that the approaching planet, whether it exists or not, can no longer hurt us, no matter what; that today is the day for which we live, and so soon we can not remember or speak at all about the occurrence of the approaching planet hereafter or at all, nor would would we wish to, remember having ever. All future threat, we agree, must be an illusion.

It follows therein, too, that we shall never again to recognize a need to think about or certainly disclose the process of installation of the ceiling, nor retain any impression whatsoever of what alien terrain our outdated societies might have once theorized could have existed beyond its edge, as it no longer has an edge now, no longer has any feature but to have always been as it now is, the way a miracle requires no corroboration with eternity when actual fate is on the line.

Such that when the new moon rose to fill the place of where we'd lost the old one, it was without fanfare, another night like all the rest. This was how the moon had always looked, we knew, covered up almost in full with advertisements, the largest of which was for the group that owned the very ground on which we stood. There had never not been a moon like this in any version of any history.

+

No child is born during the November of this year. In long white halls the youthful obstetricians stand with arms down at their sides, attending not to queues of patients bringing new faces to the planet, but to a sound inside their own unending Face, the very Face they have woke up with behind every day now for as long as they've acknowledged having life, going on without the question of what the cells had been before they took hold to form the mouth, the eyes? The hair growing off their heads like waiting wires, feed out from their skulls into what else. Each instant, as it passes, becoming that much more difficult to remember to associate as touching with the instant just before it, and the next instant to come.

What children do already exist within the present, as we regard them, begin speaking less and less, later and later, their vocabularies stunted in favor of a new range of expression they possess.

"It is as if sometimes there is something inside my daughter that cannot get out and is growing trapped inside there," a mother writes in a comment on her local care provider's webHelp.

"My child was asked to draw herself for class and she drew God," another mother writes. "I do not know how I know that she knows that the drawing is of God, that it is now my duty to punish her completely, that this is the one strike against her for which she will be given a free pass. And yet the drawing is so beautiful. I feel so much about it. I want the world in full to know."

The included picture, flagged by the bots for publication in the corporation's daily Insider mailer, subscribed to by default unto billions, is of a stick figure with no facial features, hardly anything to separate it from what could be a portrait of any person. The stick figure will within minutes become the most notorious image of the next two hours.

*What is even God now?* a preacher says before his longstanding congregation during this window, standing beside a holograph of the child's God image. And the congregation only laughs, believing they already understand the absent punchline usually provided to them in the midst of sacrament, which is precisely why they came. It is their laughter alone that stands in their future memories restructured once the feds catch up and capture each and every one of those among the pews that morning, flagged as an outbreak of national security.

Because there are no books printed in the new year by subsequent mandate, the creators of infotainment-based desire turned to speaking into their own palms, hardly recognizing any sort of trait they'd spent years studying over how to form a marketable commodity from corporately compensated private pain. Every new sentence as such appears no longer in a language, but as viral waves of refuse that clogs the open air, leaking out to engorge all local skies with brutal color, free of charge for all who still might find the nerve yet to look up, and supplemented by a calming pink noise generated from our smallest fungible motions, which felt like meat more than like sound against our ears, tiring us out in lieu of want for taking a role in our own motions as from point to nearby point amid the grid we wandered amid the longest daylight, miming our workdays, which though without purpose now we could not forfeit for fear of loss of all propulsion.

Alone, inside our homes while we still had them, the light of the sole surviving website lit our brains. No one could remember who'd designed it or maintained it, or for what purpose we logged on, what semblance of interface there was at all about the color coming out of the locked-down browser allowing us to look at only it. Sometimes the light would appear gold-colored or gray-colored without any other content, while other times it would offer instructions, definitions, maps, any of which we felt obligated to obey regardless of how the instructions often made no sense—*go now and stand now in the corner and close your eyes and never open them again; the next time you fall asleep you will sleep for seven centuries, this is the end of your life; I love you and you alone and always have and always will*—while even more often the commands could not be read or seen at all, and only felt. We could feel it creeping through our orifices like a weapon, making us stronger, or becoming stronger in us, the way our muscles seemed no longer to be ours, and how components like the machines alone might live on forever in our image, the only blessing.

What windows must have been spinning in our hearts as we clicked the codes that closed the browsers for the last time before their dissolution, closed over in us like new wounds that no longer needed any elapsing before it was again as if they'd never been, no matter how completely we still felt them in our faces, in our futures, in our language as it remained. Where throughout our down-time yet thereafter, once called sleep, we dreamed of blood. Blood up to our necks and even higher. Blood in the fruit we bought not to eat but because it was so well marketed by the machines we couldn't think of any reason not to buy it even though it didn't taste like fruit. Blood in any memory of vision, screens upon screens in our outdated childhoods depicting only scenes of ruby red tidal waves of LCD, gushing out across the face of glass boxing out the rooms of our memory like sugared sacrament. Blood wherever any remnant of the experience of prior art was, oceans upon oceans floating in the open warmth that filled our skulls behind our Masks, if not the Masks themselves, which by now no longer had the means for removal, recognition; seamless as seas in which we'd drowned, yet no less itching than the way the daylight seemed to leak its way between the verboten notion of such layers above bone, soon to beget mold, corrosion, creating seizures, human ruptures by the billion.

+

I do not know what happened then and cannot imagine. I know years began to seem to pass in every day. I know every day was shorter than the one before it, while seeming longer, full of cavities, parades. Every construction promised to stand forever until it no longer happened.

And still the Universal Ceiling shone without our knowing. Its electronic program strobed waves of cold deep blue in place of darkness, striating the condition of the buildings with a wild glow, like blacklight neon in a cave. Wind blown from weepholes cut into the firmament and funded by wind engines fueled by tax dollars.

I know I love our programmed constellation of an axe. If one connects the dots to the nearest other major constellation, the axe appears to be cutting the head off of a lion. The lights that represent the stars that would be the lion's heart, burning in its chest, are a more pale yellow than the rest, throbbing and throbbing.

I know I felt I wanted you to live forever even when you weren't me, when you were my worst enemy in history, above all, because to feel you do so steeled the remaining firmament of my imagination, my ferocity of citizenship. We walked the edge of death unknown hid in our hearts, every hour only ours as much as we could stand to remain mesmerized by nothing more than skin on skin again, wire on wire.

All the tokens in our brains. The feeling of having hands alive there like the hands of someone we believed in without knowing who they were or why, the perfect image of ourselves. Each way we weren't that person was how we aged more. Every carriage full of loam and bubbles, the clicking teeth, the writhing.

I'm afraid I know the first baby birthed on the first day of the period in which birthing was again temporarily allowed had three fingers on each hand. On its back, between both shoulders, a birthmark of what appeared to be a cross, or otherwise an icon in a language lost of its context, any tongue.

And I know at first this child seemed like a miracle, as did each that appeared thereafter, each subject to a miniseries of its own, which would play only in the sky above the house that'd done the birthing, inspiring a legion of flocking believers back to source; as if there might from the new release of protocol release a legal stream of inspiration; a way to exist within the confines of our own lives in such a way that we might coexist with fund and faith in tandem, allowed again a code by which we'd flourish.

Though shortly, onward, the defects streamed like springs on infant bodies, by the batch: eight total fingers, seven, six; two toes, or no toes; ears without holes, holes without ears, no ears at all; eyes much smaller in the face than any ever, the flesh impending inward from all sides; cleft lips and mouths so cleft they must be cut upon to allow speech; no teeth, no tongue, hipbones; and soon no genitals, no exit orifices for feces, or for speech; soft and softer; pale and fatter; small and small. They will not learn to speak a language we recognize or even acknowledge, though this will not mean they aren't speaking, all and always, through and through us, through the very air in which we believe we still might breed. Behind their skin the sound will grow and fill their eyes with absolute silence.

I know the world beyond the world revolves. *Time becomes time*, it was once said, or perhaps written, or just conceived in thought and let to drift off; each the same. What really was the time before or had been ever is as crystalline as putty, a surface beyond senses to our hearts. Every day shifts away as if it had never even had a chance to happen, such as right now, where stored unseen behind the fortress of our future household no science invents new logic to describe what once would have hung profane, the final straw in a house of millions of the same, of what goes on goes on regardless, in the image of any god. Who turns the keys in the locks rolled on wherever begets no secret not already demonstrably innate, blood in the bales of flesh put down beneath the earth to walk on while the scentless eye of time unwinds.

*And I am in here, and you are also in here, yes*, the people pray, only asking with wholly open understanding what might wind above them with their eyes closed when they no longer slave to think. In beds on beds the rooms revolving as the world does, right along with it, and so the heavens, and the flies. Seas on seas in the lather of forever. Rising broken on the cusp of an old job, where in the cubicle you believe you had been born in you find another person on the anniversary of your birth, a person who looks just like you remember you had once in your seat, reading your messages, eating your lunch, breathing your paste. Seas on seas in the leather of a pleasure borrowed, burnt like blood in a cyst removed and boiled to become putty indistinguishable from rouge, so that when who awoke before you on the day of a great change in your beliefs had also changed in similar fashion, without either of you having known at all what kind of life the other led. Beautiful fireworks rewound on the horizon so many times the way they looked as backwards felt more correct than any explosion in real time, not that you could feel the rapture of that with so much ground between you and the brains of the dead where the real reactions rapped and pulled apart even what little remained of anything like what the world had been like in any account we could be reading, even as it happened, if such a story could be thought. Light over seizures as the land changed with us upon it, born because we couldn't stop the plunging.

And what grew in beneath the bile, beneath our minds. Whose cracking cavity transpired maturation in the place we'd just been standing, having moved to the window for what sounded like the calling of our voice and turned out again to be only the animals, or demolition, misheard like every sentence ever gnawed in this life or another, all the doppelgangers spent to kernels. As now the archive was the point of plummet, and the knowledge of the color of it another temporary plume like the kiss of a stranger in a nightmare you won't remember even having under the razing moonlight of our all, with no compassion and none desired.

# TAMARA BARNETT-HERRIN

*THE LOVES OF THE PLANTS*
(*after* **Erasmus Darwin**[1])


Watery IRIS[2] octopus sentience
Inky fingers, amber tonsils
The red leathered hands of my Grandmother
Leaving her wedding ring at your root.
Purple and grey hers were, heavy nodders
Counterfeit parts structure the flower
Stern and cruel in the Disney Alice garden
Rhizomes, spreaders, favourite metaphors
Of my college's sweethearted Guattarian head boy
His mum suicided yet IRIS returns her

---

1 Erasmus Darwin (1731–1802) was a physician, botanist and writer. He wrote *The Loves of Plants* in 1791 as one book of two enormous poems. The verses were glossed with long footnotes in which Erasmus gave his observations of particular floral behaviours and specified flower biology. *The Loves* was inspired by the Finnish botanist Carl Linnaeus (1707–1778) and his system of classifying plants according to sexual anatomy: how many female stamens or 'wives' and male pistils or 'husbands' a flower has. Linnaeus defined their interrelation as a 'marriage' in the 'bridal bed' of the flower. But flowers have many irregular non-binary sexual arrangements, and so the Linnean system and The Loves gave the plant world and by extension nature itself the sheen of indolent polyamory. It was a massive commercial success, as everything that has a tang of sex about it usually is. But there was still more sacrilege in *The Loves of Plants*. First, it was organised around the pathetic fallacy, enthusiastically attributing human emotions and motivations to the vegetal world (a vice unacceptable in botanical science today, though arguably it still lingers). And last, the poem endorsed the at the time scandalous vital-materialist worldview that humans came from what Erasmus described as "one living filament" which placed humans on the same biological continuum as "lowly worms." In that heresy against the creation myth a seed was planted: Erasmus's grandson Charles would, 40 years later, drop out of medical school in Edinburgh and sail into the fertile saltwater of evolutionary science.
2 The Iris is sexually organized as three parts male and one part female. The female stigma is enlarged and disguises itself as a petal, with markings that function as a landing strip for pollinating insects, guiding them into the throat of the flower and the nectary jackpot inside, coating them with pollen as it does so. Iris are susceptible to borers—tiny beetles that lay eggs on the spear-like leaves—and borers are susceptible to insecticides like Orthene, Isotox and the now-banned Lindane. These chemicals attack the reproductive organs and ovarian cycles of mammals—enlarged testicles and decreased sperm count are among many of the recorded consequences of animal experiments with Lindane. So, in attempting to control the pests that feed on Iris rhizomes we may have created aberrant creatures which uncannily mimic the sexual camouflage of the Iris itself.

From this tablet screen that's connected like you are
Vascular, crazy, invisible rivers.

Blasted trunk of HAWTHORN[3] it was your bouquet
Swann tripped out on in Proust, correct?
The one in her garden was dead-looking
Sundered, eroded like rock, nuts when it bloomed
Pink and then red like a fortnight of sunsets
The washing line hung from it, a trail of saliva
I'd had a swing there but got too big for swinging
Now the house has been sold you'll go back to slumberland
I'll watch trees here that bristle with feeders
Sounds like eggs frying, hot engines ticking
Hi-fi vibrations, held in electric orgy-like mania
Bees in their thousands and Swann in his bedroom
And me at my keyboard all held in your power.

Holy monster WATER LILY[4] you are the reliquary.
You hold the hopes of us now we face end times
And pray to you namaste, tattoo you on arses
When you are the butthole that hots up and traps us
Changes at night while we rollick inside you
The gigantic illustrious one bred at Kew
That got pulled up and splayed out, specimen alien
An ornament arabesque systemic sphincter

---

3 The Hawthorn is known as the May-tree, due to its tendencey to bloom on the 1st of May.
Climate change may well alter this pattern, in which case the Hawthorn might lose its tether to its
common name. If there were to be an apocalyptic climate event, ancient plants might be the only
life-forms to survive, and in that case all names—common or scientific—would be meaningless.

4 The Victoria Amazonia water lily is rooted in the soil at the bottom of the Amazon river and
arranges its leaves and flowers upon the surface. It is a plant of automated morphological transformation: the flower is firstly female, attracting pollinators, and then overnight becomes male as
the anthers within the flower achieve maturation and release pollen themselves (this means that
the flower can pollinate itself). So pollination means that plants have sex by proxy. Once we imagine that, we can easily imagine how a plant might experience the effects of sex after it has taken
place, its flowers blooming in a remembered echo, or how a plant might telepathically feel another
plant having sex through the magical transference of sensory impulses, embedded in animal pollinators.

What seems chaotic is all geometric
It isn't that romance opposes technique
Still you seem impossible, specially when twirling
The mothership redesign biomorph handmaiden
The answer repeated and echoed and blasted
Out through the spongey amplified waterways
"Here is the way you survive": it's a chorus
Interdependence, collusion, revival
Anarchy: we all look after each other.

CLITORIA[5] blue vine you're not a clitoris
You are a vulva. My genitalia
Split down the middle, and a butterfly stitch
Wielded by Alison pulled me together
Later with Joycelen I felt less anger
Broken and mended, my bits still invisible
I'm not really looking: the family residue
Smeared on the mirror like mucilage sundew
Linnaeus who named you CLITORIA saw everything
Yet felt no split, he was ready
And fat in his cabinet labyrinth
Pulling the strings of an empire together
Greedy old Adam, naming and naming
Looking, recording, collecting, displaying
But you aren't a clitoris are you
You're vulval. And Eve in her pressurised cabin
Unnames you, and I hold the looking glass onto my injury
And see only sweetness and bells set to ringing!

---

5 Linneus named the Clitoria vine, so-called because the flowers resemble female genitals, in an act of naughty provocation. Like many Enlightenment orderers, his rummaging around in nature was driven by a thrill in the generative power of sex. But he made sure his four daughters were not educated, except in botany—a science, he said, "even for Women themselves." Women were the only creatures to be doubly catalogued by Linnaeus: both objects to be worshipped and specimens to be dissected. They were fixed, and never mutable, or subject to the mysterious process that Marie Stopes—paleobotanist, eugenicist and campaigner for reproductive rights—would call "inherent in life"—that which "causes spontaneous change."

The front garden ROSE[6] next to your bedroom
I felt it and cut it: it's velvety, silky and then it is cellular
Suddenly celery
They grew to your window like beans to a beanpole
As if intelligent to you—like an island
Pulling by magnets the sea to its shoreline
Reactive roses, a coevolution: you and the plant
In strategic defence against mostly everything.
P talked to Albert about grafting and hybrids
And Joan brought her furious doubt to his projects
Albert and Joan both so filthy and rambling
Urinous tramps pruning prize-winning roses
Telescopes out for the comets and planets
Beady-eyed vagabond lunatic gardeners.

Bulb of the TULIP[7] what is your status?
The ones that she gave me are still wrapped in plastic
Dormant, asleep, dead yet alive
Prophecies: rot—or get yourself eaten
By nut crazy squirrels. Your torpor sits on me.
You are too fixed, it's way too heavy
I smell embalmment. I smell lies.

---

6  The flower is the reproductive organ of the rose, but the thorns are just as vital: they
are crampons, which enable the plant to climb, and they angle downwards, to stop invading
pests climbing the stems. It's only been through breeding for size and colour that the rose
has changed from an epiphytic plant which grows in amongst hedgerows and trellised
in forests to a standalone shrub. Genetically engineered roses are spliced together from
different species, which help flowers to bloom beyond their usual patterns; and grafting
different species of rose together creates new varietals with bigger flowers, strange or
absent fragrances, and more robust stems. The plant is a now a Frankenstein's monster,
sewn together from other now-forgotten plants and written into our collective imagination.
The sensitivity of the rose angling itself towards us, or to the sun, or the horizon, is an ar-
tefact—the remnant of a plant intelligence that's been partially smothered by the tinkering
and jostling of rudimentary biotech.
7  The Tulip is classified as a bulbous plant. A bulb is not the same as a seed. A seed is
an embryo wrapped in a skin. A bulb is a dwelling within which the entire life cycle of the
plant is contained—the roots, the stem, the leaves and the flower. The bulb is already complete but requires activation. The seed is still fragile and contingent.

Teeny VOYRIA[8], Mirkwood breadcrumbs
Pale little shut-ins, teens in their bedrooms
You white-hat hackers, who bloom without sunlight
And flower on the ecstatic mushroom machine
That filters the forest. Mushy with enzymes
The web of a fungus that resonates, activates
Even the deepest night-temple shadow
All there is lit and worked into frenzy
All goes inside, and into each other
Infiltrate, orchestrate, mutually aid
One living filament igniting a circuit
A dream: we cannot unwake VOYRIA
We Sunday gardeners, we promenaders
We count the gills, cautious and tender
Frightened and thrilled by her deep calculator.

Tiny, poisonous flowering EUPHORBIA[9]
Bees immune to your toxins
Make poison honey, a magical potion we
Imbibe, addicted. Your images oscillate
On our devices, inflorescences
The insects immune, the diagonal sun rays
Our eyeballs impregnate
And the pixels activate
A deeper background
That nature is evil and killing
That we put the stinger inside us
Give entry and animate
All through the force field we've folded and fastened to
Screens like tiny poisonous flowers.

---

8 Voyria flowers on the mycorrhizal fungal network also known as the wood wide web. The system ferries food in the form of enzymes and warnings against aphids or other pests and threats, perhaps by echo-location. This arrangement of broadcast signals and unpredictable exchanges model a non-human intelligence that is neither a blind machine driven by natural selection, nor a pristine brain, disconnected from the material realm. Instead, consciousness arises from embodiment, and communicative mind is dispersed across acres.
9 The milky sap of the Euphorbia Virosa is used by the San in Southern Africa to poison hunting arrows. Euphorbia Triucalli 'Firesticks' is the carrier of a latex that, if ingested, can trigger the genetic expression of a virus which in turn triggers a lymphoma. Sometimes, plants are not remedies, but only poison.

# NORA TOOMEY

## *What Belongs on a Hook*

it doesn't matter what side

there's just one sleep—

her hair stilts

       in the sand

birds and bowling pins

be the dream be the bird again

head at the fence of her spoon mouth

so much rope

the world is flames

and you are the dark arrow

packed    in it

Tijuana feet

Tijuana horns

teach me to say

I am the swan

god snaked in the moon song

# An Arrangement with Faith

oh baby, she says

would you start the car

saw two ghosts in the chest hole

you hear me

two crummy daisies

# TS Hidalgo

## Nightclubbing

Before starting to write,
I'd say long before,
and in a club just
a few
poorly walked steps
from the exact place
where Joyce's Ulysses starts,
I became aware
of Bono,
of so many creatures infesting
the Earth under spotlights
(and it's as if there was nobody there),
of 100,000 burning bikinis on the dancefloor,
of different scents of lavender or elf leaf,
or of the fact that I have a Visa and I'm thirsty,
and, now on my way to the penguins,
of the speed of light,
the inexistence of the number 9,
and the pressing need
to play the little piano of your feet
and to whisper in your ear
that your eyes
are the color of my Porsche.

# CLINTON SIEGLE

## *Acrostic*

Time is changing you
Time is changing you
indeed time is coming to a transformation in your life
memories good or bad make you
eternity is varying your life.

Is life a change in your way of life?
Sense life transforms in your life

changing your way of life
honesty is changing you
always varying you
need to convert your love
great innovations for your mind
inward change of your love
next change of your mind
great aspiration for you?

You need time to change
open hearted change
unique wholesome change.

## Love, Sex, Romance

Love her that I do
open hearted love of her that I do
very lovely whispers of, I do
eternity in a moment of love, I do

Sex coupling erotic
erotic coupling sex
x-rated coupling sex
romance is nurturing sex

oh wonderful manners of romance
memories of love, sex, romance
a time for memories a time for action romance
nice quietly affectionate romance

counting the ways I love you
eternity is but a moment in time with you.

## *Horse, pony, colt, filly waiting for a cowboy*

horse on the trail
waiting for a cow
waiting for a cowboy
traveling across a trail
pony at a fair
waiting on a kid
waiting for a rider
traveling across a circuit
colt born wild
colt waiting to run wild
colt waiting for a mustang wild run
colt traveling a wilderness trail
filly born wild
fillies in the wildness running wild
filly waiting for a drink of water
filly running in a wilderness trail
cowboy tell me this
cowboy tell me that
cowboy tell me a horse tale
cowboy waiting on a cow trail
working with a cow
working for a long time on the cow trail
fencing the wild trail
gone wild are the horses
gone are the ponies
gone are the colts
gone wild are the fillies sad are the cowboys with fences

## Valentine's Day of Love Acrostic

all that love
love
eternity of love
nice wonderful love
time is but a moment soft on love
I love
need to be infatuated in love
eternity is a moment enamored in love
silly love
Day of memories of love
all day of love,
you are smitten in love
of course love
funny love
love
open heart of love
valentine's day of love
eternity of love.

# JI YOON LEE

## *Separation Anxiety Poem*

When my baby visa was denied
Daddy and Mommy disappeared

You aren't texting back
digitally disappearing

The illusion of having your contact info
The illusion that we are in contact
like we were in our cozy bed
But your info is up in the icloud

We are only in contact
when you are inside me
My contact lens
went over behind the back of my eye
My sense of object permanence
is permanently damaged

Father father, why have you
forsaken me

Tag, you are it
Now you are my imprint
Keep on walking, wind-up duck
My messed up imprint will have me
follow the strangers

# DAVID BLAIR

## Thinking About the Bronx

"HOLY BRONX"
—GINSBERG

Even this Galleria Mall
bland, January calm,
winter comes in
flat as paint drying,
good paint, the fountains
in fake forestry cover
burbling, round pennies
on square tiles
in the basins, the whole
of the non-city freeze
shimmers on down
through skylights.
Even the rain taught
a lot of headspace,
and that is valuable
being on a subway
and next to you
people interested
in their own heads
as you were in yours,
hard and also like
a giant quilled pillow
pulled from Mayor Koch
or other giant bald guy.
Some kid who wanders
through the D trains
in a private strobe light
under the Concourse
decades ago changes

the space around him
by being that amped
in electric urine
and Poe Cottage.

Was that the young
Donald Revell? Maybe
empanada grease
and rooftop pigeons
breaking over
kids throwing rocks
far from Sarajevo
at bottles on a glacier
rock in the lease lot,
the fence top barbed
with backup mirrors,
fiery sunset behind
red Alexander's sign,
the old man calling
you Papi, one hand
on the ice walker,
the other on his roach,
then grabbing hands,
old long finger horns
not letting go
until he inhaled
with a whoosh, you
funky ass upstate hick.
People who have
been really alone
have their charge.
Whatever comes
off their wires
goes into your wires,
who swayed between
cars you felt them
going from side
to side and never

stopped going
from side to side.

The whole world
changes, but I now
think how something
does not change at all.
The way people leave
bikes chained in front
of restaurants all night,
how amazing. And
the colors of the bikes
too. A toothpaste-
colored ten speed
city bike just leans
there with its wheels
still on it. How could
that be stable? It is
though, from that thing
that causes balance,
the inner ear, scrub
with no winter coat
pulling your pants up
darting to the market
which seems reasonable,
I mean real, concentrated,
face not bleedy, still okay.

# David Alejandro Hernandez

## *Emperor*

Add yourself to a space—for instance,
One in my living room, the corner where
My wife keeps her cutting mat and straightedge with a pile
Of other supplies. There's a lamp there now
That's new, new bulbs too. It's a cozy area.
I've wanted to tell you that in Spanish
We have the word *descifrar*, lining up
Precisely with our English 'decipher', but which I
Also, erroneously, conflate simply with *cifra*—a figure,
Quantity, or total sum. So *descifrar* could mean something
Like performing a cold sum, laughing while doing it, even
Though it could turn out to be our undoing—last
Delirious act of freezing persons in the snow.

I would like to tell my wife everything. Not everything
I see yet is red and rough as brick, but will it be?
The inscription is one that folds into itself,
A nominal sign-in to the guestbook, before anyone
(You or I, or both) would naturally get up to leave.
There is also the word *añadir*, which *does* mean
Add but I have always likened more to an act of
Abolishing, effacing, probably collapsing it with
*Anular*, meaning annul (duh), and stuff along the lines of cancel,
Clear, etc. Treat all that I'm about to say like you would treat
Someone to lunch or dinner, a coffee or an ice cream.
What I'm getting at is—don't assume you'll be returned in kind;
And if you anticipate you will assume, maybe don't offer in the first place.

# Nawal Nader-French

## *In Proximity*

*and where is a woman in language?*

### 1

That to find a woman in language we must look in a woodpile for larvae. We must look for the paradoxical self; the semitone alive in the other. That is, she knows the sound of her unfamiliarity with the other which is indeed her very self beating in semitone. That is, the notes beat in survey of her slaughtered self and she discovers her self unfixed and living in proximity to a scepter.

### 2

That her scar is in proximity to a scepter. And in her remembrance of writing, she is at a renaissance of self. That is, she can taste the passage like the pastille of the scepter. That her semitones crawl through her scepter to the rotted woodpile. That the root is the organ in proximity to the self made subaltern. That it lies in proximity below the surface. That it makes her speak as a surrealist.

### 3

That she discovers the rotted word anchored to a bollard. That the world comes in close proximity to the wrapping of self in semitones. That is when we rewrite her from the root we rhyme her rotted word with scar. Where is the woman in language? Dissected at the violent act at the root. That she is there, connecting the wounds of flesh and word and she is coming like liquid glass.

*A hybrid: and how is a woman like glass?*

0

That glass is first fixed and immovable, like a woman. That she is in proximity to wonder. That the transparency of glass is a temporary trawl to a subsystem of many factors. That glass is exiled, inevitably like a woman, waits a thousand years and reshapes itself. That it exhibits behaviors of a liquid, reveals its appetite. That woman is like glass, defined within the inclusion of time. That language is a lashing that once shaped her in sentence, chants in proximity to change.

*and where is the male in language?*

4

*malum: as in evil when it does not have a long "a" and mālum as in apple when it does have a long "a"*

That woman like glass precedes identities. That she is conceived as a neuron transmitting constructions/ eventualities in identity. That, like glass, woman transmutates and disrupts power for the male construct—pronounced /mal/: a discovery/deficient performance— injurious to all and distorted. That when malus was assigned its name, it was to play on malum. That it is woman who first defines male in language. That she excises her identity by naming him in proximity to herself.

**JENESSA VANZUTPHEN**

## The mother

The mother says to the dog, love. Love, the mother says, have some
meat. It's cooked. I cooked it with my hands. I've never killed anything.
The mother says, you're right, it's been awhile since we dressed up.
Since we went out on the town with new shoes. Glitter sad affair. A want
so badly. To add a shine to the matte blue. Yes, she says, I'll take us for a
spin. The grass is growing taller each day and we shouldn't miss it. Dog,
the dog says, dog.

# ROBIN CLARKE

What is the best flower?
Aspirin.
What is the stigmata?
A sprouted coconut
in a palm.
Mom fasted for a year on cancer.
Buttercream frosting and mayonnaise
like radiant motels.
The cat who would not leave
the porch that morning,
name him Papyrus
glued to the lining of a tomb:
"Who honored me by giving me these words?"
Her favorite flower was the asp.
Her favorite hour was the harpoon's.
How long can the elephant stand?
How long can the elephant stand
on three thoughts?

## *Nothing But Legitimate* Ha Ha *Here*

Nothing but legitimate *ha ha* here—
                the Breitbart Gestapo can move on to the next door
     for their degenerate art and neo-Bolshy heresies—
              nobody here but us chickens, tumbleweeds, Apple products
(and other famous lists from the writing of
                 Bruno Latour),
       nothing attempting the exorbitance of communion
                    one's dimly aware of in tradition
whether that be of the dodgy, reactionary kind
           or the purely operatic sort garnered from visions
     of *Game of Thrones* [I'm barely kidding], I mean
             Messiaen's "Quartet for the End of Time," or the rain
that comes once a year to revive scenes of family
           in oak-shaded homes in South Orange, New Jersey — no,
   pass on — these chants, these slurs, these poems
                 are typos in the neoliberal craw,
nothing some pharmaceutical Nair couldn't correct,
           nothing "emergent" if by that you mean transcendent — no,
     pass on — just complaints, fixations, with a touch of resilience
                one wakes to see falter, courtesy of the State.

## That Sweet Spot Between the New York School and Guy Debord

That sweet spot between the New York School and Guy Debord
                              called Kevin Davies,
              the clouds of articulated labor
                            convening above an ePUB's cubicle,
      the Eugene Thacker t-shirt arguing for a sharper horror
                                  kind of like the Cure
                  did with the best of their 80s singles
                                    not to mention the sepulchral face paste
which doesn't bother me now
                  — if Robert Smith wants to go on being ancient until
                    he's got sweat patterns on his sheets
                                        in the shapes of future album
covers, rasps as he walks up the stairs and has glass
                              knees, the music still stands
        as glimmer within the pall of adolescence
                  in the bantering cat howls above the emergence of traditional
(or classical, whatever) strings in the post-punk
                        studio — that arrival's made complete
              when, downloads later, it's purified of the reticula of industry
                        that made it never ruinously matter — though now, it does.

## The Obsessions with Freedom: Two Spaces

The obsessions with freedom: two spaces
        after a period, curls of yellow in a painting
     by Van Gogh (pronounced American style), offensive senses of humor
          baked in, like tattoos on a pig, and thoughtless affairs with members
of the opposite *Partei*—just as crystals
       of sand collect in the swim trunks to fake
         a statuary testicle, the syllable fans clones of itself (banter as form
            of gentrification), despoils numbers, reaching finally beyond
anything truly active (or whatever it was
      J. L. Austin was writing about), erecting its own spike to heaven—the very lack
         of sensual integrity causing the crimp that is
            *event*, the second-time farce of the mishap called *clinamen*—
in the likes, the Goya-cons, the "hash tag poetry," is the cost
         of a "theological science fiction" ( Jameson) bleeding us
      of love and envy, the smarter emotions, leaving only a trivial
        Treadwellian corpse, clinquant roadshow of the mind — something erotic
is missing here, we know it by the dust, the new standard of thinking
        doled out in thimblefuls of spit (not to sound didactic): the
    spell-check, the reality cop show, the Roomba, guiding us through a haze of exceptions:
        the superior rubbernecking of the tyro impatient with flux.

# WENDY C. ORTIZ

### PROJECTION 1

I evoke a tied tongue. I am some kind of sexual assassin carrying bombs. I know how to use knives and harbor an array of them in my night table. I have thick hair, strands strong enough to choke with. I'm kind of feral sexy but it's not about the looks.

### PROJECTION 2

I am an earnest and warm listener. I have answers. I know some things because I'm nearly twenty years older than you. You forgive when I don't have answers, when you're aware.

### PROJECTION 3

I'm a witch but with wings. You survey me and call me beautiful. You remark on my work in what I imagine are whispers. You steer clear, disappear, reappear. You want me to know you but you remain out of reach. I appreciate that.

### PROJECTION 4

I have it easy. I have some kind of mysterious life that you don't totally understand, so you fill in boxes. I have magic you find elusive. I am sometimes wicked. I am easy to talk shit about.

### PROJECTION 5

We are in a relationship. Somehow we know we are meant for each other though it's never said. Ever. We like everything about each other, even the parts we don't understand. We understand enough. We are also each of us old enough to know that fantasies are preferable to reality.

### PROJECTION 6

I am aloof when with you. I am bombastic elsewhere. This is noticed. This is judged quietly.

## PROJECTION 7

At times I am benevolent but you've witnessed my forked tongue and are left with questions about my intentions. I appear unfazed by your conflict in feeling about me. I always extend warmth to you, you are easy to love, even when I have conflicted feelings about you, too.

## PROJECTION 8

I am not: Latinx enough, lesbian enough, bi enough, queer enough, young enough, sexy enough, tough enough, down enough, intellectual enough. Yet I remain in your mind's eye for some annoying reason.

## PROJECTION 9

It's too painful for you to acknowledge me directly, so you tweet about how much something I've written has impacted you without tagging me, like you're speaking to a crowd I'm a part of, never once looking at me.

## PROJECTION 10

Warm energy transfusions flow back and forth between us. Softness. There's safety and nourishment here. There is no reason to be afraid.

## PROJECTION 11

You notice that I don't give you the attention you get so easily from so many others. I am not of interest, except as a moth that gets in, flutters by a light bulb, then finds a place on the wall, still. I am always watching.

## PROJECTION 12

Honestly, it's such a relief when there are zero waves of sexual energy being emitted, when we can like each other, appreciate each other's sense of humor, and no one's pants get tight or wet.

## PROJECTION 13

Who is this bitch, you wonder, who came out of nowhere…well, somewhere… you did notice me, but I was always on the periphery and now…well, who is this bitch?

## PROJECTION 14

You're on another level. Another tier. Another planet. You prefer it this way. When we meet you do know my name but after you write it once you trust I am no competition and go back to giving face to the ones who actually matter.

## PROJECTION 15

I don't exist since the day you decided I don't exist. Your friends know otherwise.

## PROJECTION 16

We have watched each other for a while and it's before I bring the drink to my lips that I already know you'll admit your crush. You know to take the lead with me, do. I disappoint you with dumb face emoji replies that I send while smirking.

## PROJECTION 17

You can't decide if it's me who's changed, you who's changed, or the landscape we're in front of. Either way, you like me well enough, there's nothing to fear, it's friendly, but you're learning you must carry a minimum amount of mistrust on you at all times. You fold it into a tiny square and put it in your pocket when we talk.

## PROJECTION 18

Is it because you also talk dreams and jump from deep subject to deep subject, rapid-fire neuronal blitzkreig while under the influence of copious amounts of alcohol? Or is it a base pheromone? I decide it's inconsequential and you feel that shift over thousands of miles.

## PROJECTION 19

I'm a fucking bully. I'm a low-key ruiner seeping ruination. I'm getting what I don't deserve. I'm a sham. You can't stop looking.

## PROJECTION 20

I approve, adore, pet, like, heart, laugh. I might be judging you but you don't see it. It's hard to know what people are really *thinking*. You know you're interesting to look at and you know you say interesting things. I can't stop looking.


## PROJECTION 21

I said the right things, surprising you, and you don't know how else to be when flattered. You want the gossip to be the right kind. It's not. In fact, I'm onto you. You eventually tell yourself I never meant what I said, especially when I don't heart all your selfies.


## PROJECTION 22

Please let's just get sauced and fuck. We don't have to tell anyone. But then how would either of us write about it? Forget it. Impossible. You text me something inane and I understand completely.


## PROJECTION 23

I have all the time in the world. I give in abundance. I am the recipient of so much luck. *Oops*! I mean I am the recipient of so much talent. You ponder this as I (probably) go hiking under a glorious sun with nothing else to worry about or do today but write and be free and do and wear whatever I want.


## PROJECTION 24

I was no one, was someone, you invited me to things, then I was no one again until you retweeted me. It doesn't matter how I feel about you because why would it? I suppose it's possible I could see through you...but who fucking cares? I don't have the beauty power or money, *bitch*!


## PROJECTION 25

I am warm. I am effusive. I am nurturing. I am old. I am ancient and it's questionable if the things I know are even still relevant but something compels you to listen anyway. You're going places and it helps that I stay in relatively the same place.


## PROJECTION 26

I was never who you imagined I was after all. You're sorry for everything you shared with me. I am beyond a disappointment. You don't like the word 'evil' but you have applied it here and there to my nature. I'm not worthy of your tears but I can't convince you of that.


### PROJECTION 27

I am not an intellectual or an academic. I've made it clear. You don't even have to spend another moment on me, won't.


### PROJECTION 28

Our secrets are bound up in one another's to the point that we are mute about one another's existence. My name has no place in your mouth. There is nothing you have to say about any of it and you forget/remember/forget that I am capable and desire to say everything…in my own way.


### PROJECTION 29

I am so far outside the lines you want to bring me in. I am indeed a little feral and you like that. I'm a test and I'm a marathon. You signed up before I even knew what was happening. I'm a test. I'm a test. I'm a test.


### PROJECTION 30

How is my keel so even? How do I get from Point A to Point Z so fast? How do I seem to have everything under control? How is it that so many people like me? How is it that you can't have what I have?

# BC Griffith

## Big Gay Ass Poem

On a train coming home from work, my butt brushes the stomach of another man.
The train is crowded, & he is standing behind me.

In this moment, the contact feels alluring:
given the crowded train, the heat, the molding yellows of the train's interior.

A voice behind me calls out, "Hey man, c'mon. You don't need to rub your ass
   up on me."

Then, "What are you, gay?"


     +


At first I wonder if what I've done commits me to the life of a sexual harasser.
Except it isn't me that rubbed the man's stomach; it is my butt.
My butt, the sexual harasser.

I think about the life that a sexually harassing butt might lead.
Rubbing itself on every surface that stimulates. A doorknob.
The flat, warm surface of a rock in the sun—
enjoying its warmth the way a sexual harasser might—
as indicative of another's hidden being,
forced into contact with my butt.


     +


I think about the question the man asks me—Are you gay—and its answer—yeah.

I think about the unusual truth of it—
the predicament the insult creates—

how it lugs itself through its rhetoric;
the only answer appropriate to this question is—
*no.*


+


Is the comment more hurtful to me because:
    A) In the casual way in which anyone speaks to another
        on a rush-hour B train, he means to hurt
        using the lowest bearing fruit one man can lob at an other.

        I am the lowest bearing fruit.

Or is the comment less hurtful to me because:
    B) To hurt me in this particular way, with these particular words
        have followed me around,
        like a kid brother
        all my life: half its own person,
        and half me through mimicry.


+


The man, disgusted by my ass, burrows his way into the crowd.


+


My ass is unmovable.
It is a gay ass.
A hot luscious piece of cherry-picked gay ass
best described by gay men with an emoji keyboard as

You are a peach, big gay ass, but
you are also a sexual harasser.

+

I think of all the places my big gay ass might have placed itself in that
    subway car, at that time.


Why there, in that man's stomach?
Had the big gay ass been attracted to the man?
Felt the need to rub its big gay assness into him?
The man isn't my type—having too large a beard, but


        +


perhaps the big gay ass is lonely.
We both are.


        +


The big gay ass had moved into the man's stomach to make room
for a woman, wearing a sunny yellow cardigan hanging loosely from
    her shoulders.

Although she wore it gallantly, cape-like, she herself seemed sad.
Sad woman, shrunken into the cardigan
like a sun turtle pumping its choad-like legs cautiously across a lawn,
ear holes peaked for a dog bark, the swish swish of a lawn mower.

Perhaps the big gay ass wanted to make room for the woman
with her pretty cardigan who seemed shrunken into the train wall,
amberized like a mosquito in midflight.

The big gay ass, which just that morning had seemed to fit nicely into its pair
    of ash slacks
but now seemed to push against them, using the big gay thighs as leverage for
    their escape.

+

Had the big gay ass not rubbed into the man at all?
But rather grown into the man,
spreading its big gay assness like a climbing ivy might?

Was the big gay ass getting bigger—gayer—all the time?


Like a gremlin from the movie "Gremlins",
perhaps this big gay ass drew gayness in,
then doubled.


+


When the big gay ass & I waddle off the train, onto the platform,
and then slip through the door into the greasy New York night,
a group of small straight children seem to swirl around it

drawn towards it, but on their way elsewhere—
swirling with such coordination,
the big gay ass and I might be Marilyn Monroe atop a subway grate:
me, pressing down my hands to keep the big gay ass from sight,
the kids bunching and flaring around me.

Then their father walks by,
saying to his wife,
"creciendo."


+


Creciendo, big gay ass,
Thy Name is Creciendo.

Creciendo-ing like two loaves of warm brown bread
left to cool in the sun.

Creciendo and I pass the closed down gas station on our way home,
the gas prices now so old, they suggest some bizarro-America,
where the gas was cheap and the living was easy.

The gas station, empty this morning,
now harbors a grasping dirt pile—
a big gay ass dirt pile touching everything it sees,
growing into the terrain around it.

Big gay ass dirt pile,
Thy Name Too is Creciendo.


+


The big gay ass and I walk home—
past the bodega with its skull-colored lights
the sidewalk crack that resembles a toy train,
to our big gay ass home.

The big gay ass and I take off our ash-colored slacks,
and we write a big gay ass poem,

on a night as tender as a weed-whacker
grinding into the withered earth.

## To The Reader: Twilight

There are ways to utilize the space between us
which is more than just words next to other words.
We've lost the urgency of commanding water
from the well to the white space,
scooping the blood of our tension
with two cupped hands.

We want to pool our motivations by sloshing through them—
whatever is on our minds—
whoever is in us—
is like a sword in hand,
waving goodbye as we sweep out the door.

The hymn of what is not known to us—
the hymn of what is not known,
even to us—
is felt as a type of war—

We lift our steely chin over the island—
in a technical pose of defiance.
This is our land.

Because we wish to be known, we are cruel.
Because we wish, we are cruel.
Because we are cruel, this is our land.

The crickets in the grass copy our sounds
As we slam one bootstep into the next—
Slamming one day into the next—
One body against another
makes us feel close
while still feeling dangerous.
As we stand to salute—
this forest of bones
where the forest once was.

JESSE NATHAN

## Do I Like Assholes?

I like the smell of assholes
Sometimes. Each with a unique rot,
A sough as familiar as a breeze in the peach tree,
Aroma-signature, like a style
You want to stick your nose in—
You want to lick
A delicate little realization.

## The Mine

Heavy pockets of angels,
a tax on secret milk.
The naked deciduous
sin for the cold green pines.
Conversations, calculations—
the wind is full of whatever.

## Weather in L. A.

I reeled in the cabbage of memory.
I shook the filter reasonably, feelingly.
Calves came over me. I was weird, sister.
Sponging in the pasture, I was eyes
Soaked and windblown like a strip mall.
A cupboard, tumbling up Sunset.

## Brother Pablo Picasso

What about a single word
for everything. This. In a museum
just after 1 PM, a youngish girl drops
with a cry in the Cubism room
wearing white heels and turns yellow
and shakes and she is saved
only by a woman who presses down
her chest and a man who breathes
for her, and I occupy six corners
of the terror as her chest
is crushed and pops up
again and again, this assemblage
of pain and precision, I the woman
running on the beach, I this nipple,
this hidden eye, this sky, this water,
this air, this fist of clouds
serving drink and lightning at seaside
someday in the weird future
to the girl who finally rises
and leaves this room.

# Abby Minor

## Innovation Nation

### 1. HI

Hi, I'm a new self-driving car. I drove all the way
to this poem. I love this poem b/c I ♥ collaborative spaces

where team members can work in teams to innovate and discover applications.

Hi, is it done yet? Can I touch it? I pray for the poem
to get bigger & discover life-
saving applications.

Hi, hi team! Look, this is my team. The team
is standing on a most amazing
pile of garbage, the team has redecorated
libraries for the future.

       Hi, I'm a new poet. I the poet am a team I'm applying
       to all sorts of things. Like,

look out! I'm going to apply my poem
now to gentle neighbors porch-
sitting under a drippy orange
harvest moon talking on cordless phones.

The moon is just clear
frustrated poetry student said
it isn't any color it's just clear
like a lamp.

Students at the nursing home poetry
writing group finally conceded OK, if we had to choose something
for the moon to wear

it'd be a snowsuit. Great what kind of snowsuit Well
it'd have to be a pretty big one.


## 2. BIG BLUE

Big blue
eyelashes descend.
To be blinked by a lazy cosmic blink
is the highest science & don't you think
if we were all blinked at the same time we'd go up
in cedar smoke? Possibly feminism

is how the blink would like to talk, or ecofeminism
is how the blink would like to talk in a place
that smells like wet brown leaves.

There are probably only about six or seven
ideas in the entire world and you can have
the particular color that leads
to each one of them

while the eyelashes are going up and down.
Now I'm beneath the feathers feeling better.


## 3. TRAINS

Even queer anarchists look at me like I'm an angel
of death when I suggest that maybe we can't really reconcile Christmas

with the revolution. All I'm saying is the fire isn't big enough
for me to fit my presen(t)ce in and at least we can all agree

that Christmas is basically *libidinal*
*energy redeemed through the figure of the Child*, so maybe Christmas is just

like feeling sort of sexy but also sort of weird
about the world and so even though

you thought you wanted to have sex actually you just want to cuddle. Sex
can be disorienting but do you really want to ride a sparkly snug electric

train around in circles forever. Zzz. You can answer that honestly. "You'd think
they'd keep them off" said Soft Black

Jacket Person on the downtown
E train looking at Red Sweat Suit Person asleep on bench. Ye rich-ass

people ye fragile, ye eyes burned by sleepy
black legs stretched out & based

on overheard whispers ye don't even know
how to use NJ transit. They been through it. You'd think they'd keep their eyes off.

In the realm of seasonal mystical demi-gods I can think of about ten thousand
other ways off the top of my head to experience Imagination & Wonder. For example

like if a giant bearded yoni came up your dish drain every summer. She goes away
with granola crumbs in her beard. The kids love it they want to know

if the yoni is real I say of course can't you hear her chewing? For a long time
I was terrified of Jesus because of what people had done

to me and felt about me in his name. Riding the E train with the sleeping man
and the wincing ones I suddenly felt washed

in the light of knowing cause I knew
the eye of God grows black

and blue. Later I put my dollar bills down for a living man
who was not the child of a deity in the long lit

underground and said God bless you before he could say
it to me and he said Woo, look at that. I wanted to high-five and say Inflation! but

it wasn't the right time for a joke. Later
I realized I should have made a joke because it's like sharing

bread. The whole situation
wasn't exclusively serious. In the tunnel it was given to me

to know that Jesus is my sibling. Jesus uses
they/their pronouns. Jesus is a menstrual goddess. I still hate the cross.

Not in the time that is coming but by the time this poem is over
I will need to reach deeper stores of feeling and will need to understand

and experience that which I have not yet experienced
and understood. I believe it would be impossible to do this

while celebrating Christmas. In the time that is I will reach my deeper stores
by standing in the circling

dark electric eye and watching Prince.


—WITH A LINE FROM LEE EDELMAN

# CLAIRE MEUSCHKE

### *the scent of herbs is a plant screaming in flames*

just when you remarked to yourself how temperate
                                                water feels
a little white snake wraps around your calf
                        a pattern of stable vortices
cinches its jaw to its own body
                the snake is heavier than its visual mass
you try to swim up to the river's surface
but your head sinks with the thought of fangs

the snake could be a metaphor for the patriarchy
easy now          a simmer
                                or an oil pipeline leaking venom
                                        into the Missouri River
but for now the snake is very much a snake

no one tells you how lonely drowning is

the secret to painting a convincing glare

add rosemary flowers at the end
collect droplets on the lid for neck and face
when you realize all your metaphors are literal examples
when you could be you or you or me

wasn't that you who
when all the children cried
put your face up to the dead rattlesnake

the rattler you kept
in a ziplock later moved to the closet to the trash when
                                                embarrassed
water boiling is the maximum freedom in a pot

*stare at forest green to get cochineal on the page*

kids say mermaid hair          staying too long in a lake
algae saturated    comparing strands to be most attractive   slimy
boy pronounced      mosquito with a maw sound in the gazebo

a new age woodsman with a pet bobcat approaches     says that's tits
                                                    to every remark
                                            neutral to good

                        hard plastic cups smell burnt
                        between red and transparent
Yosemite printed on objects

                        in half assed cursive

feeling bad for mules and donkeys who stay in the pen
                    while horses go out
tie dye results
accidental colors bleed          nearly white      no swirl emblem

fireworks      I want my very own independence day

Mariposa Battalion was federally hired to make          a human
clearing  a pristine wonder              hunters green

they set fire to Ahwahnechee homes and heard the word Yosemite
thought the people were Yosemite      the word means killers

          in bronze          plaques        photos        voices over
I don't feel like talking              like I feel     I mean          voiced over

# GARY LUNDY

### *a constant sense of departures.*

i love you all very much. but i must leave. you think. about. as walking
toward an intersecting field. in the movie the two women are simply close
friends. unlike in the book where they remain lovers until one of them dies.
decipher change as fluid accidental. observational complicity. in another the
strong woman finds love and becomes unwound. anatomical sex toy. observe
how our minds play favorites without ever noticing. you talk to yourself out
of a need to be heard. claim life still interesting.

# MARGARET JOHNSON

## *All the Others are Saved*

where are you going
it does seem like must

and then we let it rest and then we make mistakes.

I must be, how have we gone, anything else
it's a lie
circle the couch of the sofa in the sunshine
I saw you, I told a story
the listeners were clear, belonged and didn't belong
welcomed a few
Shakespeare's refugees

they're following the Tar River to different views of salvation, I didn't promise
anything, all this morning
because they were all, because they were all

not changed
then we're supposed to be surprised
a heat blanket, made from rocks
now and then the sea goddess, in the morning,
the food of necessity

maybe I'm tired of you
maybe we'll never go back
they move to the farm and make art

this hand
is the broken one
this one shears sheep

# JASON HANCHONG WEE

## *Being All Kubler-Ross At Your Wake*

The first stage is cheese.
Before that is knowing
who to call for flowers.

Before that the sum of friendship and
funeral equals chrysanthemum.

First comes service changes.
Next the shucked skin stands up
and bokeh the light.

The best part is avoiding
once more the living.
The worst is the sweat.

The next is the ache
from thawing out a wet nose.
The next stage is dust.

After that is humming—
A rumor from ground control.

The comfort of nothing.
The second is sty.
Nothing changed, not really.

The hard part is the flowers
hoarse-white from shrieking.
The last stage is dance.

The third stage a trade,
the present for one sped up
and helium-voiced.

The second to last asks for nothing
that a ghost will not deserve.

I wish, meaning I regret.
The first stage confounds—
Sometimes the wound's first.

Later comes the flame.
In the stage before the deal
is off; cinders rage.

The following is patient,
is kind. The next is sick
as taut applause.

We've been abandoned to the gods.
Our dancing spun us down the mountain.

The first stage replaces
all verbs with 'fuck'.
This stage ends with ash on bone.

At some stage you were born.
The next stage is wine
and crackers, the plain kind.

The first stage is cotton.
After that is soaking up
the spill and the stain.

After that the ground continually breathes
like the near-drowned pulled to shore.

First comes the sermon.
Next the ghosts line up
to shake your hand, one by one.

The worse is the chill.
The best part is their shadows
resemble first snow.

# Amy Lawless

## *Sex at a Funeral*

We were just cuddling affectionately. I guess you could call it spooning, but there were boundaries. After all, we're friends. I said something cutting, per usual, and he nuzzled my back like a cat. I kept talking—about what I can't remember. He then planted a kiss on my lips. I said Wait no we're at a funeral. You have a girlfriend—this is so wrong! As quickly as I said this, we are fucking. I'm on top and I peek up, he was complimenting me—imparting thoughts like goddess or freak—and I wanted to hear and remember these compliments completely. But then I remembered we are still at this funeral. And it feels better than I ever expected it could. I use my hair. My hair was really long—way longer than it is when I stand before you today. My hair was a sexual position; I'd send it ahead of me to feel his body with. I'd wrap it around and around him, he was my moth, and then I rolled him out of me like we were bowling. I felt thankful, but also more connected to him. Then I looked up and saw a giant statue of Apollo, Greek god of Poetry and oracles and sun and light. And I'm like shit. This can't get better. I was also vaguely trying to remember whose funeral it was, but I can't, so we switched positions, and we're kissing, and I kept looking back at the statue through fine wisps of my own hair. Traditionally Greek, with the arms open and pointing like he's directing traffic, possibly modeled after Apollo Belvedere (ca. 120–140 AD). One foot solid in the ground, the other pointing down into the ground. Symbolic of the fact that you know, I'm here but also not here. His hips were checked kinda sexy, kinda captured in motion. His legs were rather like trunks of old growth trees. And where does this god do his thinking? And how does this statue direct traffic, gesticulate where he is? A blue cloth draped around his shoulders. I notice little details, the way we talked about in my lucid dreaming workshop, how time had weathered the form. The statue was gross, dirt on marble, city grime on marble, time on marble, smooth. How my grandma's bathtub and this statue had similarly exposed stone filaments. I have no idea how I'm still dreaming and still fucking. We kissed deeply and I felt things here in the dream that I feel and had felt in real life, I'm embarrassed to say, but I'll tell you—really this dream is what I'd wanted for a while. They call it wish fulfillment on the internet. But finally I saw and felt in his dick and in his eyes that this, too, is what he wants. He's the one every horoscope has been about for years. Is this funeral over? he asked and I say it's almost over. And then you have to go back to her. He replies I know I know but I want you. I say It's too painful.

Then I turn over and doze, and when I wake up he's sent me three emails. In the first one he told me that I'm a brilliant writer. In the second one he told me I'm a goddess who rocked his world. And the last one, well, I kept clicking and clicking on, and it never opened. I kept clicking on it and it would not open. I keep clicking. The statue was huge and wide. I stared at the draping cloth, its royal blue light in my hands. A royal blue for an empire gone. I always find out about you before you die.

# EMMETT GALLAGHER

*Open to visitations* you're not quite sure what enters hoping that life doesn't linger
and wait gestation Δ the beginning of something unwanted the beginnings of things
wanted nothing wanted want as pain she is joyous doting you understand her more
understand lack and presence || The ending of things, the ugly wire fence in front
of the very old graveyard on the side of the highway. she texts in clusters speaks in
nonwords afraid of her own voice afraid of only certain things she does not know
afraid of how things might sound || they pinned him to the shoulder, on his back,
the other two, women, hands behind their heads on their knees she says watch
out, vehicle on shoulder but back then she said it was an object he said it feels too
subjective, he seeing his mother in that woman, she seeing who is he knew in those
running, he seeing those he knew in those running, having stolen something. The
voice as a vehicle of translation what things sound like || he was just an alligator soup
there always done to the nines he was dressed in an alligator suit they are always
done up to the nines i'm always scanning for cops you experience the appearance of
a relationship what is it shaped like was I that concerned with shape and my stillam I
still her arms in the air fixing her hair at 78 Miles per hour if you speak slowly there's
no need for abbreviation Δ The volt of vultures clustered heavy medieval faces alert
and strangely wise strangely curious strangely in the company of peace The company
of geese A quiet committee huddled with white feet she said Trait windy Tuesday go
gojhg in ift tag I preferred it to anything concrete she wanted something concrete I
never knew when I'd be turned on getting distracted by exits The numbness shuts
you off from your legs what makes you know him

# MATTHEW MOORE

## *Simone Weil Je Tente*

Pour contrecarrer une chemise d'amour dans ma peau. Pour disséquer
mentalité vous prenez une pilule de guerre civile.
Je vois votre musique dans la bataille de sept pins. Votre musique dirige des
fusils à l'adversaire.
L'argument tourné plis invisibles d'une rose blanche dans un revers blanc.
Un rôdeur obtenu à vous dans le régiment j'ai eu des semaines intérieures
avant que la première partie d'herbe ait sonné mars.
L'ennemi est apparu, chacun a su, était un parié quinella: l'avenir; enfer. Quoi
que l'ordre.
Un homme n'est jamais sacrifié, ses genoux sont tués à plusieurs reprises.
Un homme sacrifié donne de la nourriture pour le rituel, n'jamais sus avec tué
genoux, bannières de l'amour interdit.
L'argument persistent, à temps. Le monde est force habitée. Je vous portionné.
Vous me séparait.
Vous doutez que je sois audacieux. Vous connaissez parce qu'est le doute au
sujet de ce que vous m'interrogez.
Amour audacieux d'axe. Une mouche ou un ongle sous le lustre de la guerre. Dans
n'importe quelle direction
Je veux de même mettre le feu pour vous. L'amour est facile dans l'armée du
mauvais goût.
N'importe quelle forteresse, n'importe quelle saillie, donne au globe de
l'amour un lessivage, par les poils.
Vos yeux ont des bouquets des poils. L'armée du mauvais amour arrondit sur
un autre point lumineux.
Aucune excitation davantage avec loin. Mon soleil est lointain. La différence
d'une heure vous enchantez tou jours dans moi.
Personne ne travaille assez dur pour décrire la conséquence. Personne ne bat
le sens vers le bas échappement d'amour.
Le divin perfore. Les lignes violettes de grèves divines de la branche. Le piège
du hind je suis des coupures la branche.
Je nage au rythme de votre miaulement, ondulé avec des décisions
irréversibles. Flambez les falaises bleues, les fourches des

Femmes, visages des roches médicinales, ordures propres. Celui qui vous
  pique. Celui qui me ceinture pour avaler.
Simone, allument aux deux extrémités avec quoi que. Placez ma bouche
  marchant dans l'esprit de quoi que.
Nous sommes des aiguilles, et vas te faire enculé tout le temps. Trop de genres
  de soldats. La vie est pleine des choix.
Un café svp nous laissent rêveurs là-dessus. Sang plus tard. Le feu chauffé des
  pensées de minette. La nuit de peu dessus arrondi,
Je trouve l'armée de l'amour effectue le travail brutal. Ordres de marche de
  Simone Weil: Mourez;
Baisez-la avec une bouche; éteignez-vous la pour la nuit, l'nuit des années de
  l'amour; mourez si je dois encore mourir.
Je ne suis aucun témoin. Je ne suis aucun directeur de votre attention. Rien
  n'est dans l'oeil de mon esprit.
Elle est arrivée à m'a parlé. Elle m'a transformé en rai pour sa roue du feu.
Simone sanctionne celui qu'un Dieu laisse passage. Dieu paresse avec un
  slouch de Bethlehem.
Simone pourrait faire plus avec la vue d'un Dieu si. Simone accorde les
  sanctions avec le grand honneur.
Le génie me met sous ses genoux. Elle me tord son visage brûlant de corde.
Le génie émet. Le ton du souvenir. Sa presse de cuisses. L'opposé indique :
Clouez les rumeurs si les rumeurs sont affreuses. Puisque la vérité est
  indescriptible.
La police aux Etats-Unis est venue des armées cassées après la guerre civile. La partie
blanche d'amour-propre de la nation
Aime la police. Les blocs fermés par police et mettent en marche les sirènes
  qui bloquent la vision. La fourchette joue le plat.
L'enfer est le bruit de l'herbe rouge et bleue et de la nuit tournée au matin.
  Simone Weil que je juge.
À peine bord. À peine capable se lever. Simone lace sa ceinture sur son
  godemiché,
Qui est la couleur du vert au lever de soleil, cette tonalité est potentialité que
  doute reflète.
Simone me mettre en une pelote. Simone bâillonne la air avec de me. À
  l'envers.
Et elle aime que d'abord et me baise et éclate de rire à l'intérieur de moi.
  Simone et moi essayent
De battre mais nous sommes trop minces pour battre. Trop de fictions.
  Absorbe ma dissociation.
Elle m'appellent plat, chiffon, serviette. Elle dit font un recouvrement de celui,
  dit se reposent dans lui, dit le recouvrement il.

Je passe toute mon heure écrivant à son armée. J'obtiens qu'elle a cru : pour X
: une conscience énorme.

Pourquoi voulant que les personnes viennent sur précis les mêmes fois est une
question que je flâne à sans réponse.

Simone me met dans son oeil. Elle me regarde fixement, autour de son
endroit, par son endroit, avec son endroit. La manière

Qu'un génie lit, sa traction de flèches par tout avec l'inflexion. Un livre est. Il
passe complètement par moi. Quand vous avez

Aimé venir, vous avez aimé venir des archives d'une autre personne. Simone,
je t'aime et moi suis tendres. Sans axiome je t'aime.

Sans avertissement, l'armée de la pensée merdique. Là où je vais après est
Dieu me pressurise juste. N'importe quelle pensée

Déploie la sobriété, pensées perverses cet obstacle comment vous obstacle.
Simone, la tache des ondulés de retour. Axe de

Roue. Je ferme à clef chaque porte avec vous. Temps avec vous est non-
imposable. Je suis percepteur. Vous êtes toujours fatigué

Parce que vous battez la fluidité par vos poumons, bec de poinçon par la mue
éternelle de SPQR. Physicality hors du joint.

Vous vous donnez la vie d'un gorgon. Vous envoyez pour moi l'obscurité, où la
croix rétive du temps de récupération de gorgons. Pour couper la digue.
Pour hacher la digue.

## Simone Weil I Am Trying

To counteract a shirt of love in my skin. To dissect a mindset you take
    a Civil War pill.
I see your tune in the Battle of Seven Pines. Your music points rifles
    at the adversary.
The argument turned and was still invisible folds of a White rose in
    a White lapel.
A prowler obtained with you in the regiment I had interior weeks before the
    first part of grass sounded March.
The enemy appeared, each one knew, one was bet quinella: future; hell.
    Whatever the order.
A man is never sacrificed, his knees are killed on several occasions.
A sacrificed man gives food for the ritual, never known with killed knees,
    banners of banned love.
The argument persists, in time. The land is inhabited force. I apportioned you.
    You separated me.
You doubt I am bold. You know because doubt is what you ask me about.
Axis bold as love. A fly or a nail under the gloss of war. In any direction
    I want likewise to fire for you. Love is easy in the army of bad taste.
Any fortress, any protrusion, gives love's orb a scour, through the hair.
Your eyes have bouquets of hair. The army of bad love rounds on another
    luminous point.
No excitation more with far. My sun is remote. The difference in one hour
    you enchant any days in me.
Nobody works enough hard to describe the consequence. Nobody beats the
    direction to the bottom exhaust of love.
The divine one perforates. The lines violets of divine strikes of the branch. The
    trap of the hind I am breaks the branch.
I swim at the pace of your caterwaul, rippled with irreversible decisions. Flame
    blue cliffs, crotches of the
Women, faces of the medicinal rocks, clean filth. Whatever will stitch you up.
    Whatever will belt me down.
Simone, light both ends with whatever. Set my mouth walking in the spirit
    of whatever.
We are needles, and will get fucked all the time. Too many kinds of soldiers.
    Life is full of choices.
A coffee please let's dream on it. Blood later. Mulled fire of minette thoughts.
    The night of little round top,
I find the army of the love does brutal work. Marching orders of Simone Weil:
    Die;

Fuck her with a mouth; Extinguish you for the night: the night of years of
    love; die if I have to still die.
I am no director of your attention. Nothing is in the eye of my mind.
She arrived at me spoke. She turned me into a spoke for her wheel of fire.
Simone sanctions whatever god lets pass. God is a sloth with a Bethlehem
    slouch.
Simone could make more with the sight of god. Simone grants the sanctions
    great honour.
The genius puts me under her knees. She twists me her burning rope face.
The genius emits. The tone of remembrance. Her thighs press. The adversary
    says :
Spike the rumors if the rumors are hideous. Because the truth is unsoundable.
The police in the united states came from broken armies after the civil war.
    The White ego portion of the nation
Loves the police. The police shut blocks and turn on sirens that block vision.
    The fork plays the plate.
Hell is the sound of red and blue grass and the night turned to morning.
    Simone Weil, I am trying.
Hardly edge. Hardly able to rise. Simone laces her belt on her dildo,
Which is the color of green to the sunrise, this tonality is potentiality
    which doubt reflects.
Simone wads me up in a ball. Simone gags the air with me. Inside out.
And she loves that first and fucks me and guffaws inside me. Simone and I try
To fight but we are too thin to fight. Too much figments. She soaks up my
    dissociation.
She call me dish, rag, towel. She says make a lap of that, says sit in it, says
    lap it up.
I spend all my time writing to her army. I get that she believed : for X : a huge
    consciousness.
Why wanting people to come on exact same times is a question that I stroll
    to unanswered.
Simone puts me in her eye. She gazes me, round about her place, by her place,
    with her place. The way that genius
Reads, her arrows pull through every thing with inflection. A book is. It goes
    completely thru me. When you liked
To come, you liked to come from another's archive. Simone, I love you and
    I am tender. Without axiom, I love you.
Without a warning, the army of shitty thought. Where I go next is, God just
    pressurizes me. Every thought deploys
Abstemiousness, perverse thoughts hold back how you hold back. Simone
    any spot of return undulates. Wheel axle.

I lock every door with you. Time with you is non-taxable. I'm taxman. You
    are tired since you beat fluidity through
Your lungs, punch beak thru the eternal molt of SPQR, physicality out of
    joint. You give yourself a life of a Gorgon.
You send for me darkness, where Gorgons wayward salvage time's cross. To
    chop the dike. To hash out the seawall.

**STEVEN ALVAREZ**

## *yr automatic: walls walls*

0:00.2
0:02.7
so we went to school

0:02.7
0:05.4
was language spoke

0:05.4
0:06.4
polis b

0:06.4
0:08.0
though polis a language in order

0:08.0
0:10.0
so you want to school speaking on the
stand

0:10.0
0:11.7
polis a how did that

0:11.7
0:12.8
listener

0:12.8
0:15.2
can't remember past

0:15.2
0:18.2
starting polis a school

0:18.2
0:22.0
our caller polis a

0:22.0
0:27.1
polis a

0:27.1
0:30.8
autopilot mortgage financial life

0:30.8
0:33.8
all walled

0:33.8
0:38.5
what did you notice that school terms of
the languages these

0:38.5
0:44.9
what ronald claudio did you notice
anything this

0:44.9
0:48.3
polis a forty dash everything's tied

0:48.3
0:50.5
it's slightly more class

0:50.5
0:57.5
subversion on one of the law

0:58.4
1:04.4
one of the redirection tried a future of
polis a cohort

1:04.4
1:07.8
clerk abortion forward to polis a from polis
b

1:07.8
1:13.9
crystals hurdle her work

1:13.9
1:17.0
microscopes you find a car wreck

1:17.0
1:19.1
recognition

1:19.1
1:24.4
chivalry carter called record

1:24.4
1:26.1
but look great uses


1:26.1
1:29.7
first for trade

1:29.7
1:34.1
they're not occur carlota

1:34.1
1:36.9
for corporate readership corner
1:36.9
1:38.3
you open the door

1:38.3
1:41.7
polis a looks great

1:41.7
1:44.8
will go where the hole where

1:44.8
1:47.5
trip uproar

1:47.5
1:49.8
apart after work at home opera

1:49.8
1:52.2
called rashad

1:52.2
1:55.5
sure drones course for rehire

1:55.5
1:58.9
luxury literal

1:58.9
2:03.1
lunchtime reduction combat report abt
polis b

2:03.1
2:06.5
go directly

2:06.5
2:07.8
microcode talk

2:07.8
2:10.0
local wall logo or or

2:10.0
2:14.2
quatro pro where aircraft relocated or
or

2:14.2
2:18.0
perk he elected to draw upon that you
what was that the other kids who had
to

2:18.0
2:19.7
do that as well

2:19.7
2:21.7
she wanted to

2:21.7
2:25.5
what he did you get only polis b
brackish

2:25.5
2:28.4
it was not chilled in the class to
didn't speak

2:28.4
2:30.0
golfing trip

2:30.0
2:36.7
props for global

2:36.7
2:39.6
after a while polis a pioneer

2:39.6
2:44.8
shiitake abt to launch a comment for
people coral hopeful by lunch award

2:44.8
2:47.3
medical treatment at all

2:47.3
2:48.7
which will run

2:48.7
2:51.1
how long that happened for

2:51.1
2:55.5
a powerful bomb

2:55.5
2:57.8
five months

2:57.8
3:03.2
happens to yr polis behind it

3:03.2
3:07.9
starts school here you'd speak polis a

3:07.9
3:10.1
what abt yr brothers

3:10.1
3:14.8
no going to see that nobody

3:14.8
3:21.8
she starts more useful concern

3:22.4
3:25.0
when i was little something early on so
i did read

3:25.0
3:27.2
matter too much to me but

3:27.2
3:28.5
living with him

3:28.5
3:31.8
nice teacher needlessly despondent

3:31.8
3:35.4
& i think she was biting acts as
bilingual & she got me in that bag

3:35.4
3:41.7
issue polis a like me have something to
surface future polis b kidnappers teaching

3:41.7
3:43.7
do you what you want to do

3:43.7
3:46.5
westward

3:46.5
3:48.2
everybody else's

3:48.2
3:51.8
was speaking to speak & i went in with
yr talk

3:51.8
3:54.0
not going to be done

3:54.0
3:57.3
soliciting that they were doing

3:57.3
4:01.8
& i was in a different polis on the
other side again

4:01.8
4:07.2
told me & then i wd tell us tonight
are you going to the polis

4:07.2
4:08.6
polis b teen moms

4:08.6
4:11.4
speaking people in

4:11.4
4:14.7
at both the polis a border may be different
in
olympics thing to us

4:14.7
4:17.3
people that came out here

4:17.3
4:19.2
so i just want to be

4:19.2
4:21.4
no one & two

4:21.4
4:26.8
brown book we will be read polis b dialect

4:26.8
4:28.4
became a school

4:28.4
4:30.6
route that you still read to you know

4:30.6
4:32.1
replacements

4:32.1
4:34.9
i studied attorney

4:34.9
4:36.0
so that you can be

4:36.0
4:38.3
didn't use it for you

4:38.3
4:41.8
risk using to you

4:41.8
4:44.0
it was confusing to me at first

4:44.0
4:46.1
bc of all these

4:46.1
4:52.4
is still close in on a project stuff

4:52.4
4:55.4
that kids have to talk to the kids that
you know

4:55.4
4:59.6
you seem to like it's not only talk
to you in the polis a

4:59.6
5:02.3
i wd listen today will close & see
what they were i wd say that

5:02.3
5:04.4
working what the trading with

5:04.4
5:05.9
what they were talking abt

5:05.9
5:08.7
point is figure out what they were
saying in polis a

5:08.7
5:15.7
& i think that we had that you can
invest grasp a different language
yr citizens speak their language

5:16.9
5:19.1
that might help me 'cause i was younger

5:19.1
5:20.7
what yr parents think abt you
polis a citizens we narcotize for yr safety

5:20.7
5:22.4
polis a marines

5:22.4
5:23.1
they liked it

5:23.1
5:25.1
they were very happy w it

5:25.1
5:29.8
polis b migrants they have a happy life bc i
wd help
make that sometimes & i wd

5:29.8
5:33.8
peace now

5:33.8
5:36.6
thank you arms & order

5:36.6
5:39.2
directions on them
bomb bomb bomb
walls walls walls

5:39.2
5:41.7
insects attack different these nine

5:41.7
5:45.3
appealing to the store in the house polis a of
the bc by sending you wd have to

5:45.3
5:48.2
ask you cap on that

5:48.2
5:51.1
bc it was my sister she dvd

5:51.1
5:54.1
unity they cd at that good

5:54.1
5:57.7
& i bet he was in his own their own
whales

5:57.7
5:59.6
side as i was only one day

5:59.6
6:02.9
allegedly destroyed nine alcoa happening

6:02.9
6:04.9
painted pain on staff

6:04.9
6:06.5
data testing i guess
polis a select
caption & press
up or down
to adjust its timing
& left or right
to change the duration
cancel save copy

# SAM TRUITT

*"There's a dot..."*

There's a dot
of gasoline

in each of our
eyes a rainbow

that flickers when
we open them to

the light the dead
see out of

time
    & it falls
across this

page this    throb no
moment can hold

the end
of open

# JOSH KALSCHEUR

## Picture of Health

The house I shit in for six years
contained all my priorities
aesthetics of intentionally
living in disrepair and the blemishes
of my character on which I concentrated
when I tried for and failed
at sleep. I was never too warm
to be with myself naked
across a mattress pad
or newly showered or sitting
in the center of the main room
my ball sack and penis tip
numbing from a month
of cynical weather. I felt
infantilized. The years atrophied
my arms and I approached my dining
with efficiency. The paid programming
played and figures diminished from a lone
payment to interest free opportunities.
Every week I exercised on a rug
under a bike hanging by the door.
I had heard that if I ached
a certain way I could achieve
what was beyond me.
I moved into push-up position
and was unafraid of hot air
and dust from a neighbor's home
coming up through a vent
right down my throat.
I jumped rope hoping
to become so light-headed
I'd remember myself

as an athlete whose rehearsed
movements triggered
rehearsed reactions,
who would call for the ball
on the blocks with defenders
on each hip before splitting them
and kissing them goodbye.
Last night I returned
from nowhere and planned
an evening, a staged discussion
where I created you,
an old adversary.
You discussed me
and I discussed you
and then we discussed ourselves
as a pair in need and agreed
to raise whatever we could
to be free to make our minor
plans. I played us an album
full of tri-tones and reverb
and static drone and ambient drone
and stoner drone and ropey
drone and treated church organ
drone and decay drone and attack
drone and space metal drone
and vocoder drone and arpeggio
drone and opiate drone
and acid drone then the club
house drops and witch
house drops and London house
drops and trip hop drops and pop
licks and perfect thirds and hip hop
fills and skits and gauzy highs
and mids and glitchy doom
and sampled grime and sampled
sax and sampled hiss
and sampled steel
and sampled blues and sampled
trap and sampled post rock
delay and scraps of screams
and charismatic sermon

bent into a looping glacial
wash. I took off my clothes
that had imprinted me
with marks. I was overheated
so I put on a blouse.
I draped over your lap
a heavy coat. You wanted
to settle in. You said something
pressing left your space less
invaded. You put eyeliner
on my lips and told me
it was possible to live
by just concentrating
on the smell of something
so I filled a stock pot with water
and whole spices and aromatics
and the roasted bones of two birds
and brought it to a rolling
boil before reducing
and letting it simmer for four
hours. It was your first
stock from scratch
so I told you to watch
as I dipped into the foamy top
a piece of toast and licked
a bubble and held it
to your mouth so the smell
could make you full.
As a show of kindness
you offered to clean for me
and I handed you
a metal scrub brush
and a bucket and I watched you
start in the kitchen corner
where there was a raisin,
a pinto bean, a raisin,
a pinto bean, a smashed
raisin, a smear of pinto
bean, ground coffee,
brewed coffee, kosher salt,
road salt, paprika,

cayenne, cumin,
eviscerated garlic,
onion papers, paper clips,
coupons, envelope
scraps, plastic safety
seals, blotches of dried
milk and beer, honey,
maple syrup, banana
and peanut butter
and forty five cents.
I was touched
when you leaned down
and, with your fingernails,
peeled a 1995 nickel
from a diamond design
on my linoleum.
This was a good time
for us. We were enjoying
what we had, so I thought
it was time I talk, that I start
in the middle of a story
that was worth sharing,
an experience I hadn't chosen
for myself. I had been
at a friend's house
all day when a call came
that our youth minister
was in town for the night,
had something to show us.
We congregated
in a bedroom, five of us,
and he put on a VHS tape.
It looked like California.
A group of men and women
in their twenties and thirties
pack up their things
in an RV. There are shots
of gas stations and junk
food and then just interstate
and the blurred browns
and greens of farmland

grasses. The next scene
is the first with dialogue
and a man has removed
his clothes and is laying down
in a loft above the driver.
A woman with a pronounced
fringe has his penis
between her breasts, uses them
for friction.  The man
has a toothy laugh
and holds a camcorder
directed at her and his lower
half and on occasion
the gaze will move
to his point of view
as if we, the viewers, are
the ones intimately
involved. Our minister
explained this angle
as something that privileges
and triggers imagination,
which is the set goal
of the film's creator.
Potholes affect the caravan
and delay finishing.
The camera shakes
and she is patient
for him just as he is
for her and eventually
they reach an end.
Soon the group arrives
at a cabin and hikes
into a state park
and there's a boulder
scene and a gas station
scene and a shower,
a den, a family
room, a kitchenette
and, at last, a bed. Our minister
offers his take on the mistakes
made by both sides,

the potential off-camera
conversations, discussions
of how to receive
and dole out touch,
how directors manage
blocking and spatial
understanding. He pulled
from his pocket one
of his cock rings he said
he'd intended to show us
weeks earlier. He stood up,
pulling down his cargo shorts
so they crumpled onto
my friend's dirty clothes.
He took the ring
and slid it over everything
until it rested against
his body. He then began
to work himself over
until he was fully erect
and then he stopped
and said his stopping
would change nothing,
that he could stay
there and be of use
to someone without
having to coax himself
again. He warned us
it may be uncomfortable
at first but that its effects
were safe and wondrous,
both for us and our partners,
that with a few easy tips
we could learn to hold ourselves
back before offering more
to the other person
for whom it could be
a first time or a first safe time
or a first good time,
or the person might need
extra time to fulfill

what needed fulfilling.
He also told us it was our choice
and we didn't have to use
toys or implements,
that whatever felt right
to us was right, so long
as the other person
was okay with what we needed
to get off and was getting off
themselves. I listened to him
and by listening I was learning.
My minister was blocking
the TV until we made room
for him so he could sit down
with us on the futon couch
and that's the scenery
of the middle of the story.
I turned the record over
to a seven-minute song
that was only one note
bending sharp and flat
but never becoming natural.
and I listened to you
discuss me as if I was gone.
I held you to my blouse
with one arm and stood up
to kiss the top of your head.
I had found my form,
which meant I was becoming
a better receiver of touch
and I was learning
I could say no to those
who tried to steal from me
my well of good will.

## In Every Imagination Is a Divine Body

People think my spirit is silly
because it is not
original or talented.
It is, however, important
and when it is redistributed
or prescribed to others,
I'd prefer to be notified
face to face. I'm unlearning
an obsession with coddling
first person experience.
I was corrupted with this
for all of my life until now.
I reproduced a thought
only if it was partially
touchable. Now I'm months
into recovery and self-
coping. I plug in my midi-
controller and Kaoss pad
and tap out noise and capture it
on my hard drive
so I can layer effects
in my preferred program.
I whisper to myself
what I just screamed
out loud. It's time I go
on my way. (It's time I go
on my way.) Enjoy
this beautiful day.
(Enjoy this beautiful day.)
I consider the continual
nipping and puncturing
and shriveling of imagination,
which is the rebar
of some people's
personal theology.

For years that was me.
I thought God was mere
prudence and restrainer
and inhibitor of energy,
doggedly pursuing
pregnancy with me
so I might be more
passive and full
of fear. I did not
consent and now
I am here.

# JOANNA FUHRMAN

## *Search Engine Overlord*

The dystopian surface
with the 1,000 percent cotton
lining is not enough to satiate
the present, or unmake
the water buffalo
of the past. No thumbs
needed to call off
an impractical joke.
No roof parade. No
uncomfortable topiary
helmet to ruin your
dismissive eyebrow slant.
Frenemy happy hour
for all. Freedom zucchini
fries on the half shell. Yes,
to the toe jam. Maybe to
the hot-sauce prayer-closet
electioneering headache
medicine plus one. I'm trying
to be more perfect, but instead
I'm in-between and frog-ready,
mama proof post-industrial
complex. Play that fruitful music
lost girl et al. Some days
all of my favorite plotlines end
with a woman walking into
a roof. Freedom for all, even
you squeaking your way back
into the corset narrative you
thought had been transformed.
Nope! Just sign posts here:
the activist who lights himself

on fire becomes a favorite
art-house icon and then a parody
on the Simpsons only .0003
percent of the audience
"gets." Our fingers hurt
from dialing other people's
senators. Wake up, canary face!
Time for your solo.

# TASIA TREVINO

## *Dictaphone 6—Sunset, Terry Trueblood Recreation Area*

never driven
in so many concentric circles never
been in so many consensual circles
have had nothing happened
in between to me
use my voice
as an alarm clock mark
your time buy me that my elemental
chattering you eating there's no real difference
this is untouched
this is but trimmed I can't keep
my eyes rub sand in your own
palate has changed pitch at the
color palette walk on how to run a color
pallet of my homebase I know it don't know these
colors yellow I guess John
does my face look
green bruised punch under the eyes
put glaze on your own in the
glaze comes out wrong but not so
that     I don't have a punch
bowl please I have a face

## Dictaphone 7—Late Summer, Iowa River Corridor Trail

wanting that wasn't
directly in front of me
with an apple glad
                              I was
out of place everywhere beside a tree
cracked spires rising up
a feast for great consumer
decrease from think too much
                              in Los Angeles
worried about hitting not rabbits especially
not apples the worst kind of
mileage mileage and mold-
ing fixed with directions
a drone that I thought meant distraction
but was actually mantra
                              I'm supposed to
be a container Pyrex filled with manmade water a reservoir dammed
but embarrassed I'm not even
speaking at full volume of influence

# JAMES TATE

## *The Visiting Doctor*

This afternoon about half past four I was sitting at my
desk when somebody knocked on my door. I got up to answer it
when my leg crumbled beneath me. I tried to stand, but it was
as if my one leg were made of silly putty. Finally, with the
help of the arms of the couch, I pulled myself up and yelled at
the door, "Come in, the door's unlocked." The door opened
slowly and there stood a little man in a doctor's uniform.
"You rang?" he said. "Well, not exactly," I said. "Yes, but
you need me. Am I right?" he said. "Yes, I suppose I do,"
I said. "Well, then, let's get right to work. It's your left
leg, am I right?" he said. "Yes, it's my left leg," I said.
"Well, I'm afraid we'll have to saw it off," he said. "No,
please don't. You haven't even looked at it," I said. "I
heard you fall. I know the sound. It's no good anymore,"
he said. "It just went to sleep," I said. "Yes, forever,
it went to sleep forever, and that's why we have to cut it off,"
he said. "No, not forever. It just went to sleep the moment I
heard the door knock," I said. "Are you accusing me, because,
if you are…" he said. "No, no, nothing like that. It's
just a curious circumstance," I said. "Then put your leg on
the table," he said. "I don't think I want to," I said. "We're
not talking about want. It's a necessity," he said. "Who are
you, anyway?" I said. "I'm your doctor," he said. "But I only
just met you," I said. "And just in time," he said. "I want you
to leave my house," I said. "But you are a sick man. You
need help right now," he said. "My leg is beginning to wake up,
I swear it is," I said. "You only wish it were. Stop this
silliness and put your leg up on the table," he said. "Please
leave this house right now, I beg you," I said. "Not without
your leg I won't," he said. I picked up a lamp and crashed
it down upon his head. He dropped to the floor unconscious.
My leg was fine, back to its old self again. Then I picked him
up and dragged him outside and dropped him in the gutter.

## Married to the Wrong Man

I said I was very sorry for all the trouble I had caused
her. She said it was no trouble at all. I offered her a drink.
She said a drink would be nice. We sat down on the sofa. I
asked her her name again. She said, "Matilda, just like in
the song." I said, "I've never known a Matilda. That's a great
name." "My mother always wanted to go to Australia, but naming
me Matilda was as close as she got," she said. "Why did you
save me back there?" I said. "You looked like a good man," she
said. "Thank you. I just got my hair cut," I said. She laughed.
"I think I'd like you even without a haircut," she said. "That's
very generous of you," I said. "I just speak the truth," she
said. "Always?" I said. "No, just when I feel like it," she
said. "Oh, then I'll be careful," I said. "You don't have to,"
she said. "Why?" I said. "I told you, I like you," she said.
"Can I kiss you?" I said. "If you like," she said. So I kissed
her. And I kissed her some more. I kissed her until we were both
dizzy. "That was great," I said. "Don't stop," she said. Then
I took her to bed. We made love most of that night, and it was
joyous. When we woke in the morning there was a thunderstorm.
She said, "I have to go." I said, "Why? Wait until the storm is
over." She said, "I can't. I'm married." "Oh," I said, "that
makes a difference." "I'm sorry," she said, "I should have told
you." "I guess it wouldn't have happened then," I said. "Probably
not," she said. She reached in her purse and pulled out a revolver.
"And now I have to kill you. I'm sorry," she said. "I won't tell
anyone what happened. I promise," I said. "It's not that. It's
that if you're here I'll want to sleep with you again. I really
like you and I can't risk that," she said. "Why don't you leave
your husband?" I said. "I can't. We married for life, and,
besides, he's immortal," she said. "He's what?" I said. "He's
immortal. I know, I've tried to poison him three times and I shot
him through the heart twice. It doesn't bother him," she said.
"Also, he's terribly jealous and has a bad temper." "That's
a shame, it really is, but you don't have to kill me. We can
tell him we're just friends," I said. "But he knows when I lie

to him," she said. "Okay, shoot me," I said. She aimed the pistol at my head, and then said, "I can't do it." "Why not?" I said. "Because I don't have any bullets," she said.

## $119 Million at Auction

"The art world's description of me being sexless and mummy-inspired really hurt at first," says the original model for "The Scream" painted by Edvard Munch, "kind of an emotional castration." Amy Goodman nods. "Abstract expressionism has distorted generations of people," she offers in a knowing tone, then: "I want to show this clip from the National Museum of Wildlife Art where your painting was recently exhibited as part of a travelling man versus nature retrospective." The clip shows a scene of some 300 museum-goers in a line that appears to wrap around a hillside. In ankle-supporting hikers, Democracy Now!'s Rocky Mountain correspondent keeps pressing the mic at people questioning why they'd pay high dollar to see "The Scream" which is on tour in fifty U.S. cities to raise money for a land trust and some grouse. One male viewer explains: "I had seen that shit on t-shirts so many times I just had to check out the original." The girl who's with him goes "I wouldn't usually come here – it's just buffalo and prairie grass paintings – but this is cool, like Banksy kind of cool!" Along with these are patrons who dress less casually and own public land.

Goodman asks The Scream, whose real, Norwegian name is Roar, to respond to the clip. "I really have become something to everyone," he admits, "And it's important that I stay abreast of what people are saying about me, but with Google and all the social media, it just became too much work to keep up with my ever-shifting public identity." "So it was during this U.S. tour of the painting that you made yourself known to the public?" Goodman clarifies, empathy wincing through her parchment-taut visage.

"Yes, the expiration of my copyright has caused some," he pauses, "hardship, though I still believe all people deserve the chance to be in the presence of truly masterful art." "So you didn't mind being a tattoo or on t-shirts where your physical form was given to stretch, or worse, masked in a burst of burrito juice?" "That is a great question Amy, and no, no I did not feel disrespected in most of the 20th century.

With that amount of relatability I could kind of disassociate from my own image. At least at the beginning, it felt good to be so embraced while not responsible for the meaning I accrued." "So please, and I know this might be difficult, could you talk about what made you finally come out, as it were, and let people know there's actually a man behind the face? I understand quite a few health organizations used you as a sort of logo." The Scream is nodding, resurrecting some trauma inside himself, "I didn't want to let anyone down,"

he admits, "I know as well as anyone that art is only as powerful as what the viewer makes of it." "Takes from it?" "Yes, that's right, or at least that is eventually how it came to feel. It wasn't the pico de gallo as much as the insistence that I represented so many things, and not just to one person but to many. The best way I can say – it's how a smartphone would feel if it had a soul!"

Amy closes her eyes, taking his pain, and letting it nest momentarily in her royal blue blazer.

As the segment draws to a close Amy is giving The Scream a final 30 seconds in which to chronicle the environmental movement as it relates to The Scream's introjection. And he's elegant, a real advocate for the natural world with his "…orange push of light waves at smog-laden sunsets…the constant pooling and evaporation of reserves…" and as he speaks he is putting his hands up to his face, and just when he might have screamed, to show us that he is the voice behind all the meaning, he simply rubs his temples and talks on about bridges, so many bridges, so much light rail.

## Watson and the Shark

*I.*

Burgundy is roses' favorite color. Yes, all of them
The last time you were bookish, there goes Baltimore
it's a bird, it's a plane, it's two polka dots in a field
drunk on a younger the river keeps
balance is one to ensure a think
Love isn't a human right no matter how much you scream your head off—
    baby cakes
Lenny ran it over, and we haven't unloosed a phillips since
housewarming, housewarming bring anything but a groping racist
my apologies still live with game fowl
went in a skirt, came back in a gorgeous
to look at their spines repeat
feel like I've swallowed too many thermometers
take algebra and multiply it by phosphorus
just put it over
cobblestones to make the clippity-clop
I'm going to flour you up, puff
they were all Samoyeds until we were up to our throats
so tired of the JFK shooting
takes one to environmentalism
spending four days away
except justice
a little train of inspirational posters bluesy backgrounds
scratching elbows seems vacant hardened
grass is Hebrew
glade he brought you


*II.*

Listen, a plastic excavator wouldn't bother to
know she was your daughter
We put -anator on things and relax. Re-fucking lax

if a pergola shows up
we were tiny about each other
No amount of drama is going to bring the mountain back
fart fart fart fart fart fart fart \ fart fart fart fart
bifurcated wasn't isn't
The last time Terry-JoAnn dusted that shelf
To stroll is to really understand a pastry
the great collection of hemming and hawing
property disturbances and requires protection
Pete!
are running with the ivory
deer meet
when you pulled out of the driveway Rae Armantrout turned into a squid
only one is needed for success
contract, contract, contract
You see what did do it there, leasing myself to like peanut butter
maybe it's aces, but he got himself
a gargoyle with a jelly addiction

# Desirée Alvarez

## *Portrait of a Spanish Mexican Maid*

Knock, knock, Velázquez. Can I come in?
I'm standing behind the man at the door. On the threshold
wearing my mantilla and cotton peasant dress.
Will you put me in the painting with the rest?
I'd like to warm my skeleton hands
in the heat of Las Meninas.
It's so brown in here I might be in a desert
or a forest. Or be a woman from Mexico.
I might finish the canvas for you,
show you what we gave up,
how we filled the sacrificial bowl
with blood and with vision, with giving and with taking.
I was thinking jaguar, I was washing paws.
The spots do not come out from a garment of eyes.

## Stichomythic Sonnet

Diego Velázquez: Suppose I put myself in all the portraits with horses

Frida Kahlo: Suppose you put monkeys on horses

Velázquez: Suppose I visit your land of pyramids and tombs

Kahlo: Suppose the paintings on the wall of *Las Meninas* are of Aztec warriors

Velázquez: Suppose the painting I am painting in *Las Meninas* is of you

Kahlo: Suppose the Indians visit Spain first, putting kayaks in at Cadaqués

Velázquez: Suppose Dali makes lunch for you all at his villa

Kahlo: Suppose surrealism is caused by colonialism

Velázquez: Suppose the urge to paint is the same as the urge to conquer

Kahlo: Suppose the urge for war is a miscarriage of man

Velázquez: Suppose it's the urge to pray

Kahlo: Suppose it's the urge to prey

Velázquez: Suppose autorretrato

Kahlo: Suppose auto-da-fé

# Dear Conquistador, We Already Invented the Wheel

The wheel beside me is a clay toy.
We sit together underground wrapped in skulls.
Mostly what I sense are bits of shell
still reeking of the brine of home.
I was made of clay too, by hands that believed
strongly. I can still feel their warmth
shaping my face and skin, the urn of me,
yearning Tlaloc of the wind, of the painted rain,
baked in sun. Who is to say I am not a god
all these years below earth? Surely not the ones
who came by boat and made us graven goods.
We knew all about velocity and we rejected it.

# NAT SUFRIN

## Bet You Do Better In A Hat

My love lives far away but I live farther.

It is not enough, you know, to speak of summer.

This summer, like last summer, we never made it to the beach.

Every day what was the self floats farther & farther away until there's nothing but the World's Fair, on display for all modern goblins.

Meanwhile, the remains settle for dropping at the speed of light down the black hole of the New York Water Color Club.

For many of us screeds, this is home, concinnity be damned, scry the asshole if you must.

Is that possible? I mean, to move at the speed of light in a black hole?

I don't know but what I do know I never describe in detail.

Walked around Blue Cliff, made love to a headless Buddha.

The way she held her hands, let me pry them apart, sat with me.

These woods are ours, she said, & we took them slowly, eyelids percolating.

When hemlines lifted, sockets emptied, or so the saying goes.

Not truthful, however, to speak of sayings in an age of surveys.

Open, open, open, singing the same short song over & over & over.

Useless to address this directly, the holes in the bones, the skulls in the pockets.

# ∑*moon flood*

        2 peeps pass
unacknowledgedunsung
                                    knees bouncing
                                                        what
            colors
flying


miss everything


            lips
            could have
            eyes
            could have

cheeks          o           hands       o           neck
                            o


                                                all they have
                                                when they beyond
                                                *tha bunny jump*


                        ariel blazing ginger
                                buddy you tippy-toe
                        too rising barely
            clapping flickering
                bananas become
            brown pollock
                    self reeks
                            shit shit
                    shit shit
                god alone
                        this this
                this this

## Histogenesis

Soldiers at dawn.
Mists arrive
Suddenly, beat
Off slowly. I
Want a lover
Who wants a
Lover more than
Me. Antelope
On the beach
Raging. Tell me
Where to go to
Sieve without you.
Fluorescent light
Much prettier
On the tongue than
The ceiling.
Somewhere in the
USA a
Jungian weeps.
I should comfort
Him, let him teach
Me martial arts,
Bleat apart the
Ligaments of
Masculinity
One by one. Snap
Crackle Glock. One
Day even men
And women will
Let men cry. Can't
Say a thing
About the
Ocean except
Go. Now and then
Soon. No shame
Being an
Indoor kid just
Depression.

Basically
In lieu of
Sitting still, we
Went into a
Frenzy and this
Made all the
Difference.
Predicting the
Past from a
Rooftop moon in
Spite of the
Future. Hate
Reality
Because it works
So well. Love
Rutabaga
Because it waits
In the ground.
Prepared so
Many ways, called
So many names.
Neep. I dig neep.
Rhubarb crackling
In the dark.
Rhubarb meaning
Nothing meaning
Gobbledygook
Meaning put it
In a pie. With
Heat but no light
It grows faster
In search of the
Vanished light. Cruel
Farmer. The red
More crimson yet.
Harvest by
Candlelight so
The shoots stay
Tender. If this
Is not it,
Nothing is.

Freezing at the
Back of a
Bumpy Frontier
Flight from Las
Vegas, dreamt I
Danced around the
Water closet
With my mom and
Wanted to
Remember her
That way and that
Way only.
Overhead
Vowels nod, shake,
Fall to hands fall
To knees. Meanwhile
On ground no one's
Needs get listened
To. Sea above
Sky below
Equals constant
Deluge with
Nowhere to go.
Showering in
Slivovitz this
Morning, yet
Another win
Against Hitler.
In the end he
Got the artist's
Life he wanted.
To die by one's
Own hand to die
Exactly how
One wants. Bodies
Of water at
Night in the
City. Your neck
In my pocket,
My teeth in your
Sleeve. This is how

You fall in the
Ground. Not with a
Blank but a blank.
Thicket to rise.
Bound for the
Bathroom just to
Hear the sea.
Also poke the
Plastic wrap.
Inside the
Mini glass jar
A brittle pink
Geranium.
If you don't have
Anything nice
To think, don't think
Anything at
All. There must be
Some other way.
The unconscious
Useless here. The
Self, as false as
It gets. The
Chicago
River flows
Backwards more
Naturally
Than the self flows
Forwards. So
Many shapes and
Sizes if
Only we licked
More than one.
Activate Code
Copper if
Necessary.
I did much worse
Than seduce
People for drugs.
I seduced drugs
For people. Such

A sad puppy
Dog all the days
Of these lives. Far
Be it from me
To want a world
More open to
Me than I am
To myself.
*Flower is scent.*
After waves rise
They drop back
Into the
Ocean. The shore
Beckons but how
Could they. After
People come they
Drop back into
Bed. Nothing
Compares 2 U.

## In Due Time

No, not necessary. Not to go, definitely not to be

Gone. Must reach somewhere, might as well reach beyond the state line, unfazed

By the latest crystal signature. Met her in a purple shirt,

Loved her serious pout. Something about the stir of men, the sift

Of women. Pity to revise, worse to renew, begin to fawn

Commencement. To venture a grin resembling how it always was:

Everyone speaks a different language and you do not speak at

All. Someone strolled into the common room and somehow you managed.

Not bad, actually: eating pizza, discussing the skinny

Pieces, laughing at the racist firefighter. Home was never where

The heart was, except when the heart swam nude in the predawn hover

Below the train tracks chanting how good to thank God morning and night

With creatures who deny God walks the line. Moments become rumors

No one begins to unpack. He was never into field hockey

Players: Sorry. Truth with a big t exists—just one of the truths,

Hanging out, generating storage space, occasionally on

Point. Blame me for trying, monkey boy. In the end, sex sailed off and

We could not help but notice the luxury of not noticing

Luxury: forgetting what we failed to do but will do one day

When the dais falls off. To die prematurely, hungry for the

Loose beets never tasted. Turns out the song was just on repeat. What

Does it take to get there? How much is worth sacrificing? And to

Whom? God, obviously. Not dead, merely dying. The usual

Failure to thrive. Morally reprehensible to chat about

God, but not as bad as making small talk about anything else.

Forget a new password, create an old one.

# ALISON WELLFORD

## *The Women You Love*

They fall on the bed in a tangle of bodies, and she looks into his eyes, at the hazel paling along the blue. Both hands touch her face. She turns away, hides behind her long blonde hair. The moment he starts to know her, it will be the last time they meet.

+

The bass throbs through her and she shouldn't be there with him, but he wants her and she gives of herself because what else does she have to give? Her cocktail is sweet.

+

She wets her bed at night and her parents can't understand why. She's almost thirteen.

+

"Your left vocal chord is paralyzed," the doctor says.
She opens her mouth to speak, but again, nothing comes out.
"We can't find the cause. Our only advice is to rest."
She writes in her notebook: *How long?*
"We don't know."
The doctor has other patients to see. She can't write the words. It didn't really happen. If she doesn't tell anyone, it didn't happen.

+

"Thereafter, for nine days did [she]
wander all over the earth, holding torches ablaze in her hands.
Not once did she take of ambrosia and nectar, sweet to drink,
in her grief, nor did she bathe her skin in water."

+

The pain in her stomach moves from under her sternum to the left, behind the rib cage. At first it came like a knife, now a throb. Her chest is swollen where her heart is, but is it her stomach? She takes another pill. Her girlfriend will be back from work soon. She waits in silence, in the dark, for her warmth.

+

"If a man finds a virgin girl who was not betrothed, and seizes her and lies with her, and they are found, the man who lay with her shall give fifty shekels of silver to the girl's father, and she shall become his wife, because he violated her. He shall not send her away all the days of his life."

+

She takes the shears and shaves off her curly red hair. She sells it in the mail. She can almost become a man, or better, nothing at all.

+

People are smiling in the restaurant. She sees another woman at the back who almost looks like her. The woman laughs. She touches her own face, her smooth black skin, unsure of who she is anymore.

+

She no longer looks in mirrors. She never thought it would happen this way. Blood makes strange patterns on the skin. Sometimes it looks like lace.

+

The police had said that she was lacking evidence. The others lacked evidence too.

+

Xanax and red wine is better than Xanax and vodka. Cocaine makes her too nervous. OxyContin works quite well, but there's the constipation.

+

"This young nymph of fifteen is short, of a dark complexion, and inclinable to be lusty; she does not rely on chamber practice only, for she takes her evening excursions to seek for clients, who may put their case to her either in a tavern or her own apartments; her fee is from a crown to half a guinea, and she strives to earn her money by seeming to be agreeable; however, she may please some, and as we have only known her about four months she cannot have lost her appetite, but seems particularly fond of the sport."

+

She walks thirty-six miles without noticing, without a destination. She walks along highways, empty parking lots, along the railway and bus station. She wakes when the seams of her tennis shoe pop, splitting it open. She stops. Cars stream past. A diner cast in silver like the microphone of a 1950s pop star gleams in the sun. She has no idea where she is or why.

+

She throws the alarm clock out the window, something she had always wanted to do but never dared, the red plastic shattering beautifully on the asphalt below, so she throws her stuffed animals out the window, and she throws her books, and her phone, and her dirty clothes out the window, the cereal and milk, she throws her chair out of the window, and her jewelry, her photographs in the frames, and the contents of her bathroom cupboard. She puts both feet over the edge of the window until her mother holds her back.

+

"He seized her tongue with pincers, though it cried against the outrage, calling ever the name of her father and struggling to speak, he cut it off with his savage blade."

+

The phone rings again. She won't answer it. Her lawyer leaves another voice mail. She can't attend the trial. She can't let her husband know about what his father has done to her. She can't hurt her husband.

+

The walls aren't exactly real. The way the dust accumulates in the corners. The plastic light switch—that isn't real. The bad paint job. She notices how poorly it's all made, like props in a film. Behind the facades it's all empty. She can see the seams. It no longer feels like home. She doesn't belong here.

+

The shadow of the lamppost is as long as a lean man who soon will raise his fist.

+

"What can be well with a woman when her honour is lost?… She had a knife concealed in her dress which she plunged into her heart, and fell dying on the floor. Her father and husband raised the death-cry."

+

"Just hold me. Don't stop," she repeats all night long.
"Sleep."

+

"First of all, from what I understand from doctors, [pregnancy from rape] that's really rare… If it's a legitimate rape, the female body has ways to try to shut that whole thing down."

+

Running as fast as she can, her arms reach out to the trees. Green shoots cover her arms, and her legs take root in the soil. She hides her beautiful face, now shrouded by leaves.

+

"When the ancient Inachus gathered sweet herbs and offered them to her, she licked his hands, kissing her father's palms, nor could she more restrain her falling tears. If only words as well as tears would flow, she might implore his aid and tell her name and all her sad misfortune; but, instead, she traced in dust the letters of her name with cloven hoof; and thus her sad estate was known."

+

She remembers the child being born. He never cried. Not once. She breastfed him and let him go. At the time she didn't think of where he would end up, only that she couldn't bear the shame. She never had another child. She would always be the mother who abandoned her boy.

+

The same phrase repeats in her mind wherever she goes—when she kisses her daughter goodnight, when her mother phones her from two thousand miles away, when she sits down at her desk to work. "Say nothing and say it carefully," he had told her. She needs her job. She needs a home and food and health care. She needs to care for her family.

+

She sees a shaman with dark eyes and lips as small and delicate as a porcelain doll's. The shaman promises to retrieve the pieces of her soul that had been taken from her and cuts her open with her eyes. She feels it in her chest, but she doesn't understand. The shaman tells her she is covered in snakes and black tar and washes them out of her. When she gets home, she puts sea salt in the corners of her bedroom. She burns sage. The thief seems smaller, far away. She feels quiet.

+

"She builds others up because she knows what it's like to be torn down."

+

She travels to Iceland to cover her body in mud. She wants new skin, made from healing earth. The snowy landscape around her is quiet and austere. She tries to sing happy songs. It has been years now.

+

"All-powerful and ever-living God, you choose the weak in this world to confound the powerful. When we celebrate the memory of Saint Agnes, may we, like her, remain constant in our faith."

+

She touches the cold metal railing in the stairwell. She focuses on the cold. "Stay in the present," she tells herself. The nightmares have started to go away. She doesn't know why. She doesn't want to let go of the railing.

+

"Come back," he says to her.

+

"Return to me," she says to her.

+

"You are safe here," you say to her. "You are safe."
Sometimes she believes you.

## NOTES

**Your left vocal chord is paralyzed**, adapted from a classical vocalist's account as rape victim; Carrie Arnold, "Life After Rape," *Women's Health Magazine*, September 13, 2016, https://www.womenshealthmag.com/life/a19899018/ptsd-after-rape/.

**Thereafter, for nine days**, Anonymous, "Homeric Hymn to Demeter," trans. Gregory Nagy, *Harvard University Center for Hellenic Studies*, 47–50, https://chs.harvard.edu/CHS/article/display/5292/.

**If a man finds a virgin girl**, Deut., 22:28–29 (English Standard Version).

**This young nymph of fifteen**, Anonymous, "Miss L–v–r, No. 17," in *Harris's List of Covent Garden Ladies or Man of Pleasure's Kalendar for the Year, 1788.* (London, 1788), 19–20.

**He seized her tongue with pincers**, Ovid, "Metamorphoses," adapted from trans. Rolfe Humphries, Philomela, 6. 555–557.

**The phone rings again**, adapted from an anonymous Whisper app entry.

**What can be well with a woman**, Livy. *The Rise of Rome: Book 1*, "The Rape of Lucretia," trans. T.J. Luce (Oxford: Oxford University Press, 2009), 68.

**First of all, from what I understand**, Missouri Congressman Todd Akin, KTVI-TV, August 19, 2012.

**When the ancient Inachus gathered**, Ovid, "Metamorphoses," Io and Jupiter, 1. 622. trans. Brookes More (Boston: Cornhill Publishing Co., 1922).

**She remembers the child**, adapted from an account of a Kosovo war-crime victim; Serbeze Haxhiaj, "The Enduring Agony of Wartime Rape in Kosovo," *Balkan Transitional Justice*, May 29, 2017. http://www.balkaninsight.com/en/article/agony-of-wartime-rape-victims-endures-in-kosovo-05-28-2017-1/.

**She builds others up**, Anonymous, Whisper app.

**All-powerful and ever-living God**, Prayers and Devotions to St. Agnes, Saint of victims of abuse and rape, prayer card.

# LIANA JAHAN IMAM

## *At La Brea*

If eros is a love triangle, I am crushed acute. I feed girlpunk songs and lake drives and sweet potato hash to vertices as if void, as if tar pit, as if pile of shared black cotton-blend shirts ever widening and undifferentiated on bedroom floor. I am trying to ask you to no longer exist, but that's impolite. I am trying to say every day is harder and more boring. Every day is more like being part of a bone cluster, diffuse, at one with many and entirely unwhole.

If eros is a tar pit, it cannot lash wing to warn me away. Here we are until our warring mouths fill with errata: metatarsals of small rodents and slick leaves and the stray experimentally thrown sock. Until our jaws are broke open. Until we finally shut the fuck up. Eros waits on the bed while I pick up semi-mesh shirt after semi-mesh shirt. When I hold them up away from my body they make little gashes in the room.

## Or Is It Relentlessly

The backyard thick with blackbirds boring holes to the crabapples that we, too, once tried for. We tried to pie them, tried to butter and mash. We sugared and brown-sugared them, soaked them in milk, then braised. Tried to boil out the bile, the angst of those fisted things. He said it would work but it all came out bitter, nearly curdled, no sour or tart there to euphemize the slurry away. We left these things on the wide porch rail; the sun rebaked them days and days till they had a stench so strong not even the mule deer came.

Something in the soil or our dense need.

Weeks before this we drove lakeside up the Swan. At Salmon he was optimistic, pointing out For Sale signs, one on the island lodge. Our future, he said, my skin pricking up to the thought, how it hung on the spring air. He waded waist-high and I dunked, came gasping up, so cold each breath wracked out hateful, shallow, like I'd been under for years. Asking what I did that for when back ashore, sitting behind, whole body tucked round me, rubbing my arms shoulder to wrist and back again, again, again, again, so firm I felt my dry skin flake against his blistery palms. The water's pure glacier, he said. Swimming in snow.

Nobody, not one park official, asked for money that day, or anything else, for us to quit streaking yelling clambering. We were ghosts on the land, nobody but us anyplace near.

+

First summer I knew woods I was keeping house for a near-dead relative. Another pine woods, though across the country. My first ever house alone, learning all its sounds and notches.

They had legends there, one was this:
Two boys set out to the woods one falls in a crevasse a slash a hole
Second boy tries to call out pull up retrieve in the end must find help
Must leave
More men a rope some time later a boy brought up from the slitted earth
He is, by every account, a different boy than he who fell
He is, by everyone, treated as if not
A boy was lost and one found, the rest all semantic

+

At Holland we huddled close atop a picnic table, still chilled, feeding grapes to each other like he was Cleopatra or I was Liz Taylor. He made bad gags like pretending to choke on them or walking away when I asked questions about what we might do next weekend. I stayed in the shower so long that night the water turned cold, right back where I started.

And later he slept, like so often, badly beside me, rolled cigarettes in the middle of the night and went all the way outside to smoke them, backyard not porch, and I woke up like so often when he pulled the door closed behind, his woody house up the Rattlesnake so particularly noised. Though something the same, any house, state, or season, in your lover leaving bed in the middle of the night.

When I opened my eyes I saw vast dark, a dark separate from black, from night, separate from endlessness. Something with edges, chalkboard. That is to say, finite. While he was gone I wrote on it all kinds of anxious desire to which, I knew, anxiously, all our lives together he would have to respond. Maybe this was why that night in May he came back silent, seeming not even to breathe, and instead of putting hands in my hair or on my shoulders or keeping to himself, like any other night like this, he pushed one between legs and one flush to sternum, his mouth at my ear ash-cold from night air, tongue lashing. He made no sound and no impression on the washed dark of the room and the whole time, without worry, I wondered who was this man come to join me.

+

All summer in that empty keeping house and around it, the long stretches I'd go between seeing people and then how rarely, for a time, were those encounters with anyone who could place me. They nagged at me in the little general, noted my tidy purchases, garlic and lager and pre-sliced chicken breast. There were so many ways to ask a person for something.

What was it about a woman alone? Why so essential to know her origin, her every secret place. Hold her down to a process, regulation, some room or a reason. She is the element that undermines the entire system.

I spun for them. Moab, I told them. Casper. Fishtail. Places with stories so specific and impersonal they could be told by anyone.

Stories, and so questions, each day a new one, and on one such day I saw how much they knew, how many answers I'd given, weight gathering round the words. They were beginning to love me, to think I belonged to them. Shapes forming around me, almost without me and I edged them in, tacked down. By the time they asked things like when do you head back, I too believed I had some place to return.

+

When we met—or should I say, when I found him—in this slipped-in town between mountains and lakeland, gateway to nothing, he had eyes I liked, big, like the burned out grass on the hills he lived amongst. We passed a winter together in them, the hills and the eyes and some sheets yellowed long ago by camp sweat and dirt stains and whoever else'd ever been down in there, pillows marred with drool rings, stuffy north nights. I didn't have any of these things, linens or leavings, was grateful to anyone who'd let me have theirs. My lease lapsed too and I hardly told him. Or should I say, he hardly asked.

+

The drive out, westward, always ravenous and antsy besides, making futures in my mind without any real idea what ones there were to have. Only certain thing was no one back there, no ties worth cutting.
    I stopped at any sign, starting with cherry-studded cider donuts and pasties, rolling on past poutine and sweet corn and then a long while just signs reading DINER and then it was berries and peaches until back to cherries, Flathead or Rainiers, and rocky mountain oysters. Ate whenever were signs, but did learn to stop asking what.

+

When the third boy came up the first disappeared
    Might be the magician's way of telling this story

+

At Finley Point we pulled the canoe off the car and tied the cooler up and tied the sack of peaches up and shoved off and when we got out in the middle of the lake he stretched carefully out and I stretched carefully atop, moving waists aside, trying to sway tandem with the clear water I'd heard is bottomless, places. His face to my collarbone and my forehead arced to gritty plastic boat-gut. Couldn't shift enough to kiss or look, touch anything we weren't already touching, and when I came we tipped, but nothing floated off.

On the way home from that long lake day he slept I drove and at Ninepipes I pulled over, drawn by the glassy splays of marshland, the face of the moon all cut up in its reverse islands. I got out of the car, tried to stay to the trail but soon got to where I couldn't quite see the car or the way back, and I was at my shins in water thinking communion or was that the wrong thing. Wrong definition, maybe, but the right thing. Back at the car I shrieked him awake, having forgotten another person was supposed to be inside.

## Nomenclature

There's a new monstera plant whose leaves I can't stop thumbing, can't stop pushing my ringed digits through their slats, the place between green and not-green. But I don't like testing soil for moisture, what has rooted there. So  many ways to cry in the same week. Me, I cried about my breakup, about all those kids, the new Drake video, the shortness of memory. The invention of memory. All those confluences. I should clarify. When I say there's a new monstera plant what I mean is a plant that's new to me, a plant I walked past in the window of the downtown plant store for five days so that meant it was my monstera now. I should note that each time I type monstera my word processing program lops off the A. Monstera makes my word processing program uncomfortable. Monster is an acceptable, a recognizable, an organizable horror. This is a giant, multi-pronged conspiracy. It's a problem to admit this, but I love to cry.

# Bonnie Chau

## *Yogurt Code*

Once, he had lived in this apartment, once his room and my room were only separated by a bathroom. Once, I dreamed of slipping violently through white painted sheetrock and tile and exposed brick, crushing it, striking it down, blow by blow. I dreamed of growing suddenly huge and swelling up like a balloon, trampling through all of the rocks and debris, and I would arrive, ten feet over, in your room, the shower curtain dragging behind me, its rings somehow caught in my hair, urban apartment seaweed detritus. You would be at your desk, with your back to me. You would be on eBay looking to buy a truck, or tunneling into obscure online forums to discuss car parts. You would swivel around on your stool, some old squeaky thing with a small worn leather seat. Hey you would say, as if we were running into each other on the street somewhere, like that one summer I ran into you in Red Hook, and we made a lot of small talk, as if small talk were a code we were making for ourselves right then and there, exactly for this occasion, this occasion when we had receded from each other's lives because the night before Sandy hit, the intensity of the prospect of the two of us as an entity was too much to bear.

But now, years later, I was showing up in your room, not in the doorway, but in a jagged gape in the wall I had cleared, so I could get to you. After you said hey, you put aside your eBay search, and regarded me as if you could read my expression, and posture, and clothing, like they were sentences, sentences constituting paragraphs of a letter I had written to you.

I feel like a balloon, I told you. I've become huge, something has inflated me, out of proportion, and I think it was in order to get to you. You told me that one of your favorite stories was called "The Balloon," and it was all about this balloon that appeared one night in the middle of Manhattan, and what different people think about and do on or with the balloon. And how people come to terms with it, in the middle of their city lives, and the language that is used to describe it, or circumscribe it, and but the best thing about the story, was the last paragraph, because what it told you, was that it was actually another type of story, it was actually incredibly romantic because in the end it was about losing someone, in the end it had a tenderness, suddenly it pressed you up against a 'you,' the story was being told to a 'you,' who had left, abandoned the first person narrator and had now returned, and the balloon for all its explicit mystery, was actually a manifestation of an implicit mystery, that was infinitely more mysterious because it was about, you know. That's what you said then. It was about 'you know.' You could not say the word, or did not want to. I knew the short story well, and you were talking about love. It was about love. And longing, and heartbreak. I wanted you to say at least one of those words. Say it, I said, I pleaded, because from such a great inflated balloon height, I could plead without feeling small. You shook your head. I cannot, you said. You swiveled back around to reach for a jar of yogurt that was sitting on your desk. You resumed eating the yogurt, and for a moment all I could do was make deliberate observations about the yogurt, like that it was all white, and that there didn't appear to be any fruit blended in, or even at the bottom. Your spoon clinked delicately against the inside of the glass. I said get me down. This balloon-me is no good, not anymore.

You shook your head ruefully at me. I have used this word many times to describe, in my head, the way you look when we accidentally encounter each other. Every summer, for many years, we would suddenly run into each other, somewhere strange and unexpected. This shaking your head ruefully at me is a look that made me happy, because it made me feel that you felt it too, that we were stuck to each other, even if only in a parallel world, even if only in an encoded universe, that we were past the point of no return, and that we both wouldn't want it any other way.

I am not saying that I don't know better. Someone died recently, and my mother said nothing lasts forever. She said if it wasn't going to be now, it would be later. I nodded silently into the phone. I felt like this was some sort of Buddhist test, or it was a Chinese thing, to be unflinching about death, to talk about how the only certainties in life were being born, suffering, and dying. I told my mother that the American saying was Benjamin Franklin, who said that the only certainties were death and taxes. My mother scoffed. What I'm saying is that I *do* know better. Every moment you make a decision, or many decisions even, to continue on in a relationship. A relationship is work, all of it is continued, constant effort. You are never stuck to someone, or past any point of no return. There is always an out. I had loved someone once, we had loved each other, for years, and he had left without a word.

Is this what you stormed through my wall for? he asked. To tell me you had that before once? Never again, amirite? No, I said, you already knew that. I came because I ballooned, and now you're just sitting there eating your fucking yogurt, and unable to say the word love, even though it's completely removed from us in this context. He deliberately, very calmly, spooned some more yogurt. The yogurt was a precariously viscous pile with a slight wobble on his spoon. I stared at the dollop as it shivered there, midair, on his spoon. I rushed forward and grabbed his hand holding the spoon, and pushed the spoonful into his face. Fuck, he said as his chair rolled back. I immediately felt better, and more normal sized. He had yogurt glopped on his nose and eyelashes and forehead, and it was glooping down, some of it dripping, and some of it glooping down more slowly. He sat on his stool, his mouth still slightly open from surprise, and then he grinned at me and licked some of the yogurt from the side of his mouth. The spoon had ended up in my hand, and I laid it carefully on his desk, and then I pushed him back a little more, until his back was up against the desk, and then I straddled him. The scene had taken a turn for the pornographic, what was all this yogurt on his face but some sort of evocation of cum, after all, and who would be surprised that my mind dropped into my vagina at this moment? But the stool squeaked unsteadily and his hands already having slipped around me to each grip a handful of ass cheek, he stood up and lifted me up with him. I wrapped my legs around him, and licked the yogurt off his eyelid. It was plain, full fat. I wanted to say hey, that's the kind I get too, but decided against it. This was no time for romance. This was time for Streptococcus thermophiles. Once, long ago, in a previous life, in West Hollywood, I had had some sort of vaginal infection, a whole series of annoyances and pain and discharge and creams inserted, and my boyfriend at the time had started complaining about the effect this had on our sex life, and though his reaction disgusted me I still stayed with him for two more years after that. At one point, the gynecologist had prescribed probiotics, which she promised me would help balance out my flora and fauna. Apparently my vagina was a forest ecosystem, full of plant life and animals, and I was to add some living microorganisms into the mix to concoct a big party in my crotch. I think this is why even as he deposited us both on the hardwood floor of his room, I continued lapping at the yogurt, lapping up that milk and bacteria. I suspected that the more turned on I got, the more yogurt there would be for me. He lay on the ground now, on his back, and I hovered over him like an animal crouched over another animal, in a mode of nurturing and care, or of predatory intent, I suddenly wasn't sure. My pussy was pulsating, a caged creature grown too large for its enclosure, seething to get out. Sink its teeth into *something*. I swayed, the inside of my mouth tasted slightly sour and frictiony. I wiped the rest of the yogurt off his face and then brought the yogurt-coated heel of my hand against my swollen pussy. I had come down from balloon size, but here I seemed to still have some balloon left. As lightly as I could, I touched the yogurt to my outer labia shy and full, while he lay there, still, his hand now pulling his cock out, now spreading precum around and around and glossy on the tip. He watched me. There was no more yogurt on his face, now there was yogurt galore creaming at my crotch. He touched it too, the yogurt. I tried to remember what we had been talking about, I had been mad about something, there was something I had wanted to say about love. But the yogurt was driving me mad, my vagina was salivating for Lactobacillus acidophilus. It had no need for conventional yogurt pairings, like fruit, or granola, or honey. Its ability to sustain pleasure rested solely on the yogurt. Mouthful, mouthful. I finally crawled forward and positioned my vagina over his penis. I could taste it in my mouth. I wriggled around, and put the tip of his cock right there. Yogurt, I breathed, and the word now had lost its logic. Yogurt yogurt, and I pressed myself down on him, his penis pushing up into me thick and slick. Yogurt, he said, and for a gleaming moment, I swore he was talking about love.

# Steffan Triplett

## *Flood the Room*

a man tells the boy to imagine a house / one with many rooms / walls he walks past often / ushering guests elsewhere / so as to keep them / from lingering / the room right away / a room that others have trouble thinking about / or, perhaps, have already renovated / flip or flopped / he knows this room / tucked away under the stairs / at the front of a modest house / a little white door / intended for storage / & cleaning supplies / but now making space / for something else entirely

+

today he opened / his biggest shitbag / before, had only squeezed / out the air / reducing its size, just a little / only until the stench became / too overwhelming / to not seal off / but today he found himself / ripping it open, & he could see / the white plastic / was holding many mushy things / so he took it out the office / & drug it down some stairs / a sidewalk hoping / others wouldn't notice its stink / the trail of stick behind him / he slugged it / into the car / told his partner to ignore the smell, for now / he would explain another day / odor becoming sound / a one armed hug / brought the shitbag into his studio / already cluttered with its own shit / smell wafting from the sinks / set bag on carpet / hoping it wouldn't bleed / then sat on his bed / with a feeling / the bag was here to linger / the shit spilled onto the floor / to flood the room / & here he had / to cede / there was no avoiding it / he took a nap / it covered the walls

+

behind this door / there is yet another home / a home that migrates geographies / as does an exhibit of art / a display of spatial reasoning / turned product on canvas / or pages that only exist as memories / of those with a ticket / the first room / says the words that would be too on the nose to be spoken: / beware the cannibals / a bust of yourself, eyes missing / someone else's fingers / gripping the temples /

behind this door is not just a home / but a house that opens / to an entire neighborhood / interlocking streets with cozy names / inhabitants who look beyond what stands in front of them / new neighbors seeing invisible / its heart a particular street / no, a particular basement / with only one window / houses haunted without ghosts / only speaking when they have to / warning the only way out is through / your memories will eat you / alive

+

to bed / is to resting place / is to garden plot / is to dig / is to grave / is to pot a garden plant / or a flower that will bloom at night / in the morning / is to pierce / is to copulate / is to pit / one against or next to another / & another / is to ditch / is to fuck / is to prick / is to abandon / a sleeping place / is to lay out plots / in a dream / in the earth / is to go to bed / is to fall / asleep

+

when he was still a boy he travelled / to a house / called The Nightmare / & he should have known / when something shows you what / it really is / the saying still stands / for a house / or a home, put on by a church / meant to scare the hell out of you

in the first room / the home turns into a jail bus / complete with sinners just like him / felons and alcohol / zooming walls / crash & carnage

in the second room / he is forced to watch a fictional man / force himself onto a fictional woman / he wants to leave / but instead a man asks / *you like that don't you?* / the actor believing him to be as a man / & not the victim / scene ending in suicide / a gun in the mouth / thwick of the spattering blood / on a wall

the third room is Hell / or representation / men & women hanging / upside down from bars / painted all types of colors / a hissing cage / a floating up

in the final room / a bloodied Jesus / asking God / why? / the boy / no longer wanting / to be saved / by these people, in a church / water instead of prayer / vomit at the end / it all looked real / they call it spookhousing / in these parts

+

he returns to familiar / but wonders if the house has followed him / hours away to a bed / no longer his own / if a thing looks too real, it begins / to look counterfeit / it is not over / it all has no end / it always starts again

+

he is eleven again / & he thinks that maybe *this* is what makes him / that if it wouldn't have started / then he would not be / in a man / tells a therapist / also a man / he knows how this sounds / knows he's not supposed to believe / is the first time he utters it / aloud / & he is alone / & he is wrong / & he is eleven again / & twice before this he's been touched / once on a bus by a boy who thought it silly / & another time in the back of a class in front of everyone / but a teacher / students giggled / the principal called home / he cried because he was *in trouble* / his parents told him to never let anyone touch him *there* / *especially a boy* / & he is afraid that a third time will be the charm / a confirmation / so he keeps it to his-self  / & one time turns into

+

a man tells the boy / imagine a self / in a future / who has moved beyond / the pain of questions / of other men / *how many years old?* / *why let it go on* / *for so long?* / *what would you say to him* / *if you could* / *if he were here* / *in this room?* / what does the self look like / in this future? / the boy imagines science but fiction / all robots & asteroids / he an astronaut impermeable / suit & helmet / okay & filled / with air / an old dream, once left in a box / in a dusty closet / now flying in rocket / entering clouds / fluffy then all-consuming / soaring up & out through atmosphere / & the stars dazzle up close / & a friend in the moon / & the earth looks just a swirl / all water & flooding land

# DAN CHU

*Jeremy Lin*

A chink in its armor? Chinese President
Xi Jinping looks vulnerable

for the first time.
THE WALL STREET JOURNAL

At last a chink of light on a deal
for Scotland's fiscal future.
THE DAILY TELEGRAPH

Love And Hip Hop Reunion: Now that
Chink and Chrissy have called it quits,
it seems like Rashidah Ali might have
a thing for Chink.
VH1

And through Wall's chink, poor souls,
they are content to whisper.
WILLIAM SHAKESPEARE

*Dan Chu reads again to make sure. Editor?*
*Post-racial America? Post-Jeremy Lin?*
*A Chinaman in armor is pretty well protected.*
*The armor is "Made in China?"*
*Dan Chu gets it.*

*Dan Chu as a light particle, Dan Chu as a light*
*bulb, Dan Chu as bailout money! Dan Chu as*
*yellow, not green, not light, not white.*

*Chink Santana, stage name of Andre Parker,*
*plays a R&B producer and love interest*
*in a reality show. He's been called "Chink"*
*to his face more times than Dan Chu.*
*"Appropriation!" Dan Chu screams,*
*hurting himself in a jealous*
*confusion.*

*Those who died building the Great Wall*
*were themselves built upon. One day, Dan Chu*
*laid his ears on the wall's cold ground*
*and listened for his ancestors' advice. Whispers*
*began bubbling when two gweilos*

*appeared and started making out*
*with Dan Chu's prone body between them.*
*"Um...hello?" said Dan Chu, but he saw*
*and heard only tongues. The audience*
*laughed, muffling the speech of his ancestors.*

*Jeremy Lin starting in the NBA is an Obama*
*moment for Asians in America, says Dan Chu.*
*"My adopted nephew, who's Asian, didn't think*
*Jeremy was a big deal," replies a teacher.*
*Why, thank you for telling me that*
*so I can steal it for the ending of this poem.*
*Watch me flip it like Jeremy's*
*Xanga handle in middle school:*
*ChINkBaLLa88.*

Chink in the Armor:
Jeremy Lin's Turnovers Cost Knicks
in Streak-stopping Loss to Hornets.
*ESPN.COM HOME PAGE*

# TMI IRL

Tired of the feeds,
I kick it old school and step back
to the Dark Ages.
I'm a serf, growing cherries
and coriander, bound to a lord
who holds my head
in his "divinely righted" hands.

Oh scrap those quotation marks—
what makes this vita nuova
is the sincerity of not knowing:
the surprise of a courier's steps,
thy keeping of thy view of thy meal to thyself,
the hope that dance
brings rain for my cherry crop.
My wisdom teeth stay in.

*See any trolls? Or signs
of your yaoguai?* says Muriel,
a village gal I've been talking to.
We're atop a sentry tower,
and I finally see the glistening
of the twilight forest
that she's always jabbering about.
The trees chime their final birdsong
before the curtain of the moon.

A virgin on a distant pyramid burns.
*Gengie*, says Muriel,
cause I'm her Genghis Khan,
*that tribe will have such a bountiful harvest!*
I've put microaggressions behind me.
The skies will cry at the purity
of the offering. Yes, the Earth
is bigger than the sun. No more
chuckling during services.
The daily messaging soothes.
I feel like Galileo.

## Porte Ouverte - 1/16/16

# KRISTIN BOCK

## *Uncanny Valleys*

When you pass a mannequin in a store window, and she looks exactly like your mother when she was young, without hands.

When you see sand bags about your size.

When, at night, the closet door left open like a coffin.

When you run up to the edge of a cliff, lie on your belly and look down at the tops of trees for the first time.

When you see a mannequin that looks just like your father but has no sex parts.

When his face through warbled glass.

When your whole family goes hunting for garnets and the rock face looks like blood spatter.

When you have sex for the first time, look in a mirror and are surprised you are still a girl.

When something freshly torn out, twitches.

When dragged by your ankles down a rock face. When dragged by your ankles anywhere.

When no one comforts you crying in the woods and, at the same time, you are looking down at yourself crying in the woods.

When you finally grow up and just finish fucking someone you think you love, and shit pours from their mouth.

When you find yourself on stage next to a stripper barking at you on all fours like a dog.

When everyone is laughing.

When you bare your teeth like a dog.

When the tops of trees are beautiful for a few seconds, and then they are not beautiful, not beautiful ever again.

When the cigarette hanging from your father's bottom lip looks like a skinny white girl.

When you are a skinny white girl and catch your reflection in dirty toilet water.

When dragged down a rock face, not just a few inches, but the length of many twelve-year-old girls strung together.

When you dream you are being crucified on a mountain and look down on the roof of your home.

When dusk casts a green light on your veined hands.

When years later, peeling eggs in the kitchen, a bleating goat startles the afternoon you thought you were happy inside.

When you can no longer tell if you were ripped from the trees or the trees were ripped from you.

When a maddening fluid takes you by the ankles.

When your hipbones are peeled eggs.

When a bleating goat.

When the animals of the forest swivel their eyes and ears away from the direction of the cliff.

# SERENA SOLIN

## Exposed Fragments of Sculpture

"I had no desire to make a megalithic monument…"
—NANCY HOLT writing in *Artforum*, April 1977

**Nancy, a sparrow demands an audience.** Everything is where you left it last night. Gravel pricks your feet. Wait. Reeds clutch the screen door, choke the bridge to New York.

Nancy, close the door. Even concrete lets sun in. Letting sun in, an idea you were born with. Huge heavy video camera. Scrambled eggs over hard. Work after this work. The earth of the lab is steel. The eye of the lab is glass. A microscope makes you love what you put on slides, but quietly—how the small parts strive.

Nancy says she will learn to drive stick so she can go to Europe.

Nancy flips through photos of a cowboy graveyard.

Nancy, "for the love of gaudy and Gaudí."

Nancy, "attached, a terrible drawing I did of a mountain."

Nancy mails a birthday card "with love from both of us."

"Nancy, you know what you're doing."

"Nancy, you're wasting my time, Christ, if you wanted to be part of it you should have just said something."

She will make a home in the desert with the pattern of stars inside it.

+

**Robert,** listening to wooden flute, sudden laughing attacks, cutting glass, plagued by

192

insomnia. Robert, learning the inaccessibility of the countryside of the soul. How to get to it. Learning he might not get to it.

Robert, always, would rather not move: "I am just now having a run of good luck here."

His heart is clipped to his breast, ready. A yellow cab skimming the slick can't help looking like a burst of sunlight. *It is only in isolate flecks that / something / is given off / No one / to witness / and adjust, no one to drive the car*

+

In 1968 you and Bob went to Las Vegas with Michael Heizer, "ravaged, needy, fierce, suspicious, witty, loyal, sly, and pure," and a dear friend. Michael performed hating New York with the enthusiasm you had come to expect from him. His projects were distressing in their scope and brutality. By the next year he would be showing a piece in which he had miles of land dyed with highly flammable, rotten-smelling aminos.

It was your first time in the American Southwest, your youthful discovery of the flank of the country, unrelenting as a held drone note. You lived out the week in ecstasy. You told Bob all the winter nights you'd known were windowpanes with fingerprints on them. Nancy, I worry about friendship constantly. It is the only way to survive unless one alone can build shelter. But there
exist huge sandy dayscapes in the reds and shales that keep us as a people enthralled with Mars, and here the sight of any other person is shocking.

You had no family west of the Appalachians—here we differ—but you did have "2 engineers, 1 astrophysicist, 1 astronomer, 1 surveyor and his assistant, 1 road grader, 2 dump truck operators, 1 carpenter, 3 ditch diggers, 1 concrete mixing truck operator, 1 concrete foreman, 10 concrete pipe company workers, 2 coredrillers, 4 truck drivers, 1 crane operator, 1 rigger, 2 cameramen, 2 soundmen, 4 photography lab workers, and 1 helicopter pilot." As with all the projects you and the others were working on at the time, a substantial crew was necessary.

It was assumed that if you could have done the work yourself you would have preferred to, no need for the delegating and reviewing and waiting around (which Bob, Michael, and the others professed to hate but stood around doing nearly all day anyway, their shirts unbuttoned to the waist and sticky). But you loved the splitting of the work, the idea broken down to tasks, never executed exactly the way you asked for. In grade school you sent a letter with the description of a monster to a student in another district, and the picture she returned to you was more fearsome and colorful than you could ever have drawn yourself.

Bob said that words had material properties and it was so rational, so ambitious. You smoked a little more to get the visuals going, then leaned back against his knees. Once, as a child, you saw a man walk into a stop sign and bounce off it horribly, his head vibrating like an alarm clock. Despite yourself you laughed and laughed. Of course words are like that. Fully three-dimensional.

+

**In the backyard Bob buries glass, buries any corner of the sky he can capture.** He wears a somber, workaday expression to complete the jetty, which establishes him as major. He pulls *Island of Broken Mirrors* after a month of nasty letters from the environmentalists. The *Times* gives him little, reluctant praise, barely concealing their smirking. He shrugs instead of snapping when Oppenheim rags on him a little. The shadow of a helicopter passes over his face.

Most days when you come home he is in the living room with someone, or someone and a smoothskinned lover/student, speaking fluidly. Your house is not a laboratory but O tinkling glass, O tinctures sweet as molasses, O discoveries, always someone else's. If you occasionally tire of Robert's gnomic tendencies, you are not alone.

With a friend's child you race marbles, rooting for this twisted red one, this striving green one, its ribbonheart suffused with blue. But why? the child asks. And by whom?

*Scrambled eggs over hard*

it happens in the time it takes to separate
his portion from yours, which you prefer runnier

a few seconds
turning them over on the heat
until they are stiff

it was meant
to be a late lazy noon in July
a short pass in a small jet

over Amarillo

Finish the ramp, with help from Carl. Maintain upkeep of the jetty until it is finally swallowed by the lake. Get a PhD student who didn't know him in to do the cataloguing. Write the people working each site and tell them their jobs must still be done, done even better. Keep appointments with a host of biographers. Answer calls and letters from the men. Keep up with their exhibitions. Finally sell his parents' house in Rutherford. Give away the long lambskin gloves balled up at the back of the dresser for years. In the summer visit the soon-to-be site of *Sun Tunnels*. Write Richard back saying yes to the video. Buy more pillows for the daybed at the studio. Bathe. Read the book someone got you about staying sane the first year, and what happens after.

+

Pick up new pants for the party. Try to figure out where to send an apology after missing the party. Design a stone nook a mountaineer might climb into, where safe, warm, enclosed, he might watch snow sleet sideways. Talk to a librarian up at Columbia about the papers. Meet with the lawyer a few times about the will, though essentially nothing about your financial situation has changed, and the insurance payout will be sizable. Wait a while to receive it while thinking on a parcel of land in Arizona. Send a little bit to Campbell. Or is it Randall. Write in large letters on the check **FOR RENT ONLY**.

+

Get a taxi instead of a rental car. Catch another taxi, hotel to dinner. Catch another taxi from the restaurant to a bar. Stay inside the little rented apartment the whole day after. Travel home. Start to lose a sense of being contained in your body. With M and D it happened just as fast and no one faulted you. Imagine a firm bed in the sand. Make an appearance each time you sense
they've finally forgotten you. Change essentially nothing about the house except what must or they'll look at you sideways. Nip the fleshy belly of a dumpling and let the soup burn the roof of your mouth.

+

I slept feverishly on the journey    I was sick   I woke up and we were in Utah
the windows of the houses          knocked out to make the dwellings          nontaxable
someone explained     Nancy I called to you as I slid      down the desert like oil in the dark
pipe      beneath it     I was six weeks into a new medication      for my skin      requiring
monthly blood draws      and a regimen of contraceptives          I was fourteen years old
unpregnant     specifically warned against      becoming pregnant      the pill pack had
a drawing of a pregnant woman      with a big red X through her      climbing the canyon
I bled          thin air          blood in it      climbing up to my thorny sleeping spot I bled
bled again          two girls were disciplined      got   booze      from two counselors
hardly men          twenty-one if that          were not fired          the season
was at its busiest      the crevices needed guides      good      in a kayak      and
dependable on the radio          plus we all had breasts          they took the girls
to the houseboat where      our chaperones were sleeping      after that they got in cars
and took the girls somewhere nearby          or so the girls said          proudly after
no longer permitted to swim in their bikinis      there were whispers      it was fucked up
being the ones taken      and the ones to be punished      they were caught because
one of the girls told      it was handled delicately      like the deformation of my back
a grown woman simply said      you can't be seen like that      and I took the medication
a grown woman simply      said you can't be seen like that          referring to my back
referring to Monica and Nathalie's      isn't that the costume of our time      I asked
I didn't see many other options at the store          you won't be able to swim          she said
I still loved to swim      I took the medication      I said thank you      for buying me
the medication      it was very expensive      it was cosmetic and voluntary      I am grateful
I have smooth skin      I hardly take care of it          it most always behaves
in the desert air I was especially prone          to fits of bleeding          mostly from my face
inside my body glands      withering to nothing      starved of proteins      shut down slowly
Nancy I called to you      as I rubbed myself frantically with lotion      I was turning
into a potato chip version of myself      very brittle      very willing to have a conversation
with anyone      to make sure I          could still hear through the shutins of my          earways
through trickling water      and cave silence      they found out after that it can make you
depressed      whoops      it can also make you short      no      I think I dodged
that bullet      my bones feel      their appropriate size      though I was meeting smaller
and smaller women in the waiting room          a girl who played the violin beautifully
my eighth grade science teacher      they had large heads and large hands      short
legs and short arms      they looked much like the babies that had been described to me
which makes sense      one needs glands for growth      but then you have your perfect
skin      I did not feel depressed      I loved a biography of Andy Warhol      I loved
his eight hour film of the Empire State Building      they call it slow cinema      they like to
watch a train stop to collect      and offload people      I dreamt of cool green grasslands
every time I'm in the desert      I want to      I dream of grasslands      I am nervous
with a ruler in my hand      I rap myself on the hand to see      I trap myself in my hand to see
I face forward in my chair      and am not spoken harshly to      while in transit      I am invisible
I crawl into      the shade of a concrete tunnel          pricked with astrological patterns

## California

The new piece extends me
past myself, into atmosphere.
By inverting valves, wheels,

pipes, I can make myself
known in the damp air
of all the places I am.

I'm getting things done
but slowly. I look away
from the shore painted

red by the dieoff. I
wonder in the sanguine
water how anyone works

out here. California.
Land of large elevators,
bare and wide, for freight.

So many are buried
in the things they collect.

# ERICA HUNT

*from Veronica, A Lamentation...*

SOMEONE MATCHING YOUR DESCRIPTION

you wake me up, Veronica
to escort you to the door to the unknown
I am slapped awake and paperless;
my eyeglasses abandoned on the ledge
startled
a tongue triggered dry
staring into eyes emptied of the exact shape of
mercy. they are ice.

you, Veronica, are beside yourself
your face a burned down house
count
me in so I can walk with you, Veronica
though you are mostly alone

(even)
dry eyed
at your own funeral

(even)

being of two minds is not enough

when Jacob

wrestled with an angel

I wonder

who wrestles with me

or you (even)

to argue "reasonable" doubt

when I know they never leave their

guns

they carry them

in churches, bars and court rooms and put

"scare" quotes around the world


they

are never mistaken

there are no words for mistake

no words

for mistake

no reason for indefinite register

*they speak in a prose that refuses to be tamed by thought's inflection, always
mad as hornets in a front pocket, inedible, stuck on the fear of deserved
reprisal, the axe that never quite falls, hold that thread please, so they call
to quarry, prey, foot stool and chattel, someone's back to stand on, to enable
them to climb the ladder faster, unletter the ladder faster and limit equality to
a single call, a single meaning, a single tongue, a simple song for how long.*

there are no words
for mistake
no
obvious thread that binds the master
to the missing supply of mastery

(even)
sleeping history's abolished fictions
live absent the bigot
whose afterthought is our
undermine

(just)
one knowing: what is known from before
and knowing what the owners of copious knowing

know
without speaking, say without saying
exactly, "be my scapegoat, my sex toy,  my
just dessert, my bowl of candy
profits, my penciled thought, my extinction."

there's so much to do for justice, we're running out of brink. so I grab my socks and
pull them up. slip the latch on my one-track mind and avoid the chair that catches
me with a nap. I point my feet in the left direction, prove, I am all ears, work with the
pivot, the hip
the city, its dance map, avoid the cemetery of stubborn spots. avoid walks with a slow
crawl, and notice the furnished detours along the way

Each step one takes in public, jars the partially apprehended panorama of the cookie
cutter's regrets and is an occasion to learn from the field of the interior. Here. the
street home, catalog, collected histories of first aid and relief, post no bills on dread,
seek out uncollectibles, be suspicious of fancier goods lost then found, bravery starts
from the bottom in love notes warriors send souvenirs home

The simple assault of questions too numerous to canal, the sky's not the limit, it turns
out the breeze a whisper of eighth notes detached from the staff, birds wing by named
and numbered in regimented flight, no words without commitment to the act of
answering
or defaulting to an I don't know

This is where love comes in coat on or coat off, hat on or hat off, go back for
gloves, go back for umbrella, go back for scarf, for plastic orange glasses, rain
boots with frog face on the toes, they like them, the boots remind them in their
looking
for all the world's details undetectable plunge beneath scrutiny,
their small hands fitting perfectly into mine
let few events escape
marking a turned page like a bookmark
as if dropped on the path days ago, shows up later in melting snow.

# TIMOTHY OTTE

### After *Psalm 121*

```
T   O   A   S   K
W   H   O   W   I
L   L   H   E   L
P   M   E   A   N
D   K   N   O   W
T   H   E   L   O
R   D   W   I   L
L   K   E   E   P
M   E   F   R   O
M   T   H   I   S
T   I   M   E   O
N   A   N   D   F
O   R   E   V   O
R   M   O   R   E
```

T O F I N D
N O C O M F
O R T I N T
H E P S A L
M S O F D A
V I D A N D

T O C R Y
W I T H H
I M I A M
N O P E R
S O N I A
M O N L Y
A W O R M

# GEOFFREY CRUICKSHANK-HAGENBUCKLE

## Her Eyes Are a Color Capable of Sight

*Nenuphars fair cannot compare*
*Though songs thread through*
*Their silken hair*


Now, while I still have my health
& the sky is clear like an open book

I want to spill it all out on the page
Days that pass like water from a glass

Moving their lips while I speak
Here I am, overlooking the Mediterranean ...

Look at it! This world out
There drowning alone

Like a broken tree
Its balconies buried alive

*The sea wades in with its giant fists ...*

Dawn half sunk in the earth
The day on its knees

Bleeding from the knees
Brown cows browsing around the plowshare ...

## In Costumes More Illustrious Than Those of the Holy Ghost

Lilith is the phantom.
She's the phantasm when she

Appears to claim what is but in name that wife's
Child by birth, but is instead havoc's hellish offspring.

A demon cannot cross a blessèd threshold. It is
The Devil's work to see the bride is *carried*

Into the nuptial chamber. This is her "in."
Revelation piggybacks on the bride.

So these two pieces of string go into a bar.
Bartender says, We don't serve no dirty

Pieces of string in here! And throws 'em out.
The two pieces of string are sitting on the steps

In front of the bar, and one piece of string says
To the other piece of string, Let's just go to the bar

Across the street. Second piece of string says, Nope.
I wanna drink in here. Then he grabs himself by the top

Of the head, musses his own hair, ties himself up.
He walks back into the bar. Barkeep says, Hey!

Aren't you that dirty piece of string I just threw out
Of here? Dirty piece of string says, I'm a frayed knot.

Insane? Apart from those black bats, and what I came
To see as pain, my own insanity was like being stupid.

I imagined that I had a daughter, hallucinated her
in the street, talked to her, told my friends about her.

She was half Mexican Indian, of course. She had a name
Backstory, home. I related her through Mexico City

To the Balmoral in the family of Prince Charles.
Things got still more frenetic. Her family

Came into wealth through two well placed marriages
Effected for a bride who went undiscovered as a man.

He was a homosexual, but as "she" he had children ...
Everyone believed me, and I myself was certain.

Such illustrious proliferating genealogies are common
To schizophrenia. Nerval believed he descended

From Eleanor of Aquitaine. He, too, had spirit sisters.
Phantasmagorical brides. Artaud named six daughters

Of the heart, yet to be born. They had sexual relations ...
But this is what I mean by stupid. I had a number

Of five-inch-long pieces of string tied in knots, that
I carried around in my pocket. I used to take them out

To show, patting them carefully, arranging them as if
On display. I thought of them as Quipu, the Incan

Calendar cords. With what could only be an alarmingly
Unwarranted earnestness, *I presented them as my art* ...

This thing with strings is not without mad precedent.
Nerval is said to have hung himself with a hank of rag

He carried around in his pocket, claiming
It was a garter given him by the Queen of Sheba ...

## Sonnet in X

The World Soul's slow
Disrobing before the mirror
Of Forms is an image.
First blush came over your picture.
The immateriality of paradise
Lost just to look at you.
At dinner you bare
Your shoulder —

*Which alone with the lack of pale lilies is loaded . . .*

*For the Master has gone to drink tears from the Styx . . .*

*When the Shadow threatened with its fatal law . . .*

*Victoriously fled the belle suicide . . .*

*(FOR SETON SMITH)*

## Peering Up Skeletal Towers or Staring Down Into the Tail

Trakl nursed a death wish from cradle to the grave.
Are those his poems I always see on the Vassar train?
The water in the river of forgetfulness no cup can contain.

# READING

**Desirée Alvarez** is reading James Baldwin, Carl Phillips and Layli Long Soldier. Her poetry is recently included in *What Nature* (MIT Press) and this spring in *Other Musics: New Latina Poetry* (University of Oklahoma Press). She received the May Sarton New Hampshire Poetry Prize for her first book *Devil's Paintbrush* and is currently an artist-in-residence at Brooklyn Botanic Garden.

**Steven Alvarez** is the author of *The Codex Mojaodicus*, published by Fence. Next to his notebook are *lo terciario / the tertiary* by Raquel Salas Rivera, *Mess and Mess and* by Douglas Kearney, and *Lake Michigan* by Daniel Borzutzky. He lives in New York City.

**Tamara Barnett-Herrin** is reading Jim Woodring's *Poochytown*. *Deadly Words* by Jeanne Farvret-Saada, *Satanism & Witchcraft* by Jules Michelet, *Witch Craze* by Lyndal Roper and *Night Battles* by Carlo Ginzburg. Emily Mortimer's translation of *The Odyssey*. Robert Bosnack's *A Little Course in Dreams*. *True Hallucinations* by Terrance McKenna. Ursula K Le Guin's translation of the *Tao Te Ching*.

**David Blair**: "I'm the author of three books of poetry—*Friends with Dogs* (Sheep Meadow Press), *Arsonville* (New Issues Poetry & Prose), and *Ascension Days* (Del Sol Press). I highly recommend Alice Notley's *The Grave of Light, New and Selected Poems, 1970-2005*, Paul Blackburn's *Proensa: An Anthology of Troubadour Poetry*, and *After Claude* by Iris Owens.

**Kristin Bock** is the author of *Cloisters* (Tupelo Press) and is rereading *Distance from Loved Ones* by James Tate, *The Real Moon of Poetry and Other Poems* by Tina Brown Celona, *With Deer* by Aase Berg, and *Frankenstein or, The Modern Prometheus* by Mary Shelley. She is currently reading *Sarah Kane: the Complete Plays, Girl in a Band: A Memoir* by Kim Gordon, *John Ashbery: They Knew What They Wanted: Collages and Poems, The Last Man* by Mary Shelley, and *In the Still of the Night* by Dara Wier.

**Tess Brown-Lavoie** is devoted to non-canonical knowledges; would marry books by Claudia Rankine, David Wojnarowicz, Bhanu Kapil, or CA Conrad if marriage was an alluring fantasy; currently reading Brontez Purnell; honestly is still not over Ferrante.

**Nicole Burdick**: Books that have lingered in chairside piles: Lisa Feldman Barrett, *How Emotions Are Made*; Adam Crothers, *Several Deer*; Laurent Dubreuil, *Poetry and Mind: Tractatus Poetico-Philosophicus*; Zbigniew Herbert, *The Collected Poems*; Alfred L. Kroeber, *The Arapaho*; Roque Larraquy, *Comemadre*; Eric Schlosser, *Fast Food Nation*; George Szirtes, *Bad Machine*.

**Blake Butler** is the author of five book-length works of fiction, most recently *300,000,000* (Harper Perennial). His fourth novel, *Alice Knott*, will be published by Riverhead in 2019. He lives in Atlanta. Current reads and recent favorites: *The Nocilla Trilogy* by Agustin Fernandez Mallo; *Nip The Buds, Shoot the Kids* by Kenzaburo Oe; *Milkman* by Anna Burns; *Mare Piss Superkill: Sea-Witch Vol. 3* by Moss Hope Angel; *Complete Plays* by Sarah Kane; *Close to the Knives* by David Wojnarowicz; *LIVEBLOG* by Megan Boyle; *The Letters of William Gaddis*; *Alone in Poland* by Molly Brodak; *The Golden Fruits* by Nathalie Sarraute.

**Bonnie Chau** is from Southern California, where she ran writing programs at the nonprofit 826LA. A Kundiman fellow; she is currently a bookseller at an independent bookstore in Brooklyn and assistant web editor at Poets & Writers. "I recently published my first collection of short stories titled *All Roads Lead to Blood* (SFWP/2040 Books, 2018). I just read and loved Valeria Luiselli's *Lost Children Archive*, and am currently reading *Guestbook: Ghost Stories* by Leanne Shapton, and *A Writer of Our Time*, a biography of John Berger by my friend Josh Sperling. I've been on and off reading and rereading *The Agony of Eros* by Byung-Chul Han, translated from the German by Erik Butler—it's so small and thin, so sometimes I just carry that around in my bag as a backup book. Some books that have been seminal for me over the years: *The Thin Place* by Kathryn Davis; *Beloved* by Toni Morrison; *Close to the Knives* by David Wojnarowicz; *The Blind Owl* by Sadegh Hedayat, translated from the Farsi by D.P. Costello; *The Naked Eye* by Yoko Tawada, translated from the German by Susan Bernofsky; *Seven Japanese Tales* by Junichiro Tanizaki, translated from the Japanese by Howard Hibbett; *The Chronology of Water* by Lidia Yuknavitch. A bunch of more recent books that I've been thinking about a lot: Yelena Moskovich's *The Natashas*; Anna Moschovakis's *Eleanor or the Rejection of the Progress of Love*; *Break.up* and *Vertigo* by Joanna Walsh; *Love Hotel* by Jane Unrue; *Things to Make and Break* by May-Lan Tan; *The Gift* by Barbara Browning; *The Taiga Syndrome* by Cristina Rivera Garza, translated from the Spanish by Suzanne Jill Levine and Aviva Kana."

**Robin Clarke** is the author of the poetry book *Lines The Quarry* (Omnidawn, 2013) and the chapbook *Lives of the Czars* (nonpolygon, 2011). She is currently reading *Extra Hidden Life, Among the Days*, by Brenda Hillman, and *Love in the Time of Cinema*, by Kristi McKim.

**Geoffrey Cruickshank-Hagenbuckle**: "I am currently reading *Cunny Poem Vol. 1* by Bunny Rogers (First edition, hardcover, 2014, Small Batch Books) which I got for $8 from some vendor who had no clue what it was. *God with Revolver* by Rene Ricard, and Harryette Mullen's *Muse & Drudge*. My best loved books, ever, are *Maldoror* by the Comte de Lautréamont, *We Have Always Lived in the Castle* by Shirley Jackson, and César Vallejo, André Breton, Aimé Césaire: complete. I am a poet living by the apparent means of an immaculate grace. We call it dumb luck. My heart's delight is Seton Smith. My film credits include *Tremors* (Universal), *Finding Forrester* (directed by Gus Van Sant), and *Our City Dreams*, screen interviews with Kiki Smith and Marina Abramovic (directed by Chiara Clemente)."

**Leah Dworkin** writes in New York City. She is currently working on her first collection of short stories, *Hey Whitefish*. Texts that have and continue to inspire her greatly: *The Vet's Daughter* by Barbara Comyns, *Bad Behavior* by Mary Gaitskill, *Collected Short Stories* by Leonora Carrington, *Little Labors* by Rivka Galchen, *The Vegetarian* by Han Kang, *The Complete Fairy Tales* of Hans Christian Anderson, Ariana Reines, and everything Grace Paley and Kafka.

**Joanna Fuhrman**'s books: *Freud in Brooklyn* (Hanging Loose Press 1999), *Ugh Ugh Ocean* (Hanging Loose Press 2013), *Moraine* (Hanging Loose Press 2006), *Pageant* (Alice James Books 2009), *The Year of Yellow Butterflies* (Hanging Loose Press 2015). All time favorite books: Jayne Cortez (*On the Imperial Highway*), David Shapiro (*Blown Apart*), Elaine Equi (*Ripple Effect*), John Ashbery (*Double Dream of Spring*), Paul Violi (*The Curious Builder*), Barbara Guest (*The Collected Poems*), Alice Notley (*Mysteries of Small Houses*).

**Emmett Gallagher**'s Current and recent: Ed Skoog – *Rough Day*, *Anna Karenina*, Michael Ondaatjie – *Anil's Ghost*, Louise Glück – *Descending Figure*, Joy Williams – "Chaunt", Nick Flynn – *Some Ether*.

**Edgar Garcia** teaches in the departments of English and Creative Writing at the University of Chicago. He is the author of *Signs of the Americas: A Poetics of Pictographs, Hieroglyphs, and Khipu* (University of Chicago Press, 2019) and *Skins of Columbus: A Dream Ethnography* (Fence Books, 2019), from which the selection published here is taken. At the moment he is reading a mixture of new and old favorite books: Gordon Brotherston's *Book of the Fourth World: Reading the Native Americas through their Literature*, Bill Holm's *Northwest Coast Indian Art: An Analysis of Form*, Mark Rifkin's *Beyond Settler Time: Temporal Sovereignty and Indigenous Self-Determination*, and Walter Benjamin's wonderful 1927-33 radio broadcasts (published as *Radio Benjamin*).

**Raquel Gutierrez**: "I hit send before I cut and pasted my reading notes but they're essentially the new memoir by Cherríe Moraga *Native Country of the Heart*, out in April on FSG) and *We Remain Traditional* poetry by Sylvia Chan and favorites are *The Moths* by Helena María Viramontes and *The Poetics of Space* by Gaston Bachelard."

**David Alejandro Hernandez** is a first-generation Mexican immigrant born in Guadalajara, Jalisco and raised in Northern California. "For now, I'm an educator at Washington University in Saint Louis, and working part-time in other ways. Most recently, my thinking-life is enchanted with or ensconced in these books: Lola Álvarez Bravo, *Picturing Mexico*; Mei-mei Bersenbrugge, *I Love Artists*; Michael Allen Gillespie, *Nihilism Before Nietzsche*; Danielle Dutton, *Sprawl*."

**Jason Hanchong Wee**: "I often read to prepare for my art projects. I'm working on the appearance of the cannibal in explorer accounts of Southeast Asia. I'm reading *An Intellectual History of Cannibalism* by Cătălin Avramescu and *The Headhunters of Borneo* by Carl Bock. For a new manuscript of science fiction haikus on a future Asia post-Asia, I am also finishing up William Connolly's *A World of Becoming* and Teo You Yenn's *This Is What Inequality Looks Like*."

**TS Hidalgo** has currently developed his career in finance and stock-market. His first book of poems, *Construction Time Again*, will be published in April by Amargord Publishing House (with distribution in Spain and all of Spanish America). "Favourite books? I actually choose the complete works of ee cummings, Marianne Moore, Russell Edson; among our contemporaries, authors like Juan Carlos Mestre, Lawrence Ferlinghetti, Gerald Stern or Bob Hicok."

**Erica Hunt**'s *V Suite* is forthcoming in 2019. Her current stack of books include a manuscript version of *The Year of Blue Water*, by Yanyi, *The Hawthorn Archive: Letters from the Utopian Margins* by Avery Gordon, *To See the Earth Before the End of the World*, by Ed Roberson, and *Demonic Grounds: Black Women and the Cartographies of Struggle*, by Katherine McKittrick. Also Marcia Douglas, *The Marvelous Equations of the Dread*; Charles Bernstein, *Near Miss*; Terrance Hayes, *To Float in the Space Between*; Toni Morrison, *The Source of Self-Regard*.

**Liana Jahan Imam:** Recent: *Paul Takes the Form of A Mortal Girl*, Andrea Lawlor; *The Leftovers*, Shaelyn Smith; *Calamities*, Renee Gladman. Forever: *The Waves*, Virginia Woolf; *Coming Through Slaughter*, Michael Ondaatje; *The Beauty of the Husband*, Anne Carson

**Stephen Ira**: "I'm reading Aristilde Kirby's chapbook, *Sonnet Infinitéismal n°3 / Matérial Girl n°8*. I'm reading a novel, *Since I Laid My Burden Down*, by Brontez Purnell. I'm reading Diana Hamilton's new book of poems, *God Was Right*."

**Margaret Johnson** lives in Rochester, New Hampshire. "I have had poems published in *Ironwood* and *Oblek*. I have also had a chapbook, *A Visit to the Cities of Cheese*, published by Burning Deck Press. Right now I am reading *The Unfollowing* by Lyn Hejinian, *A Tibetan Grammar* by Benedicte Vilgrain, and *The Lumberjack's Dove* by Gennarose Nethercott. In fiction I am reading *The Broken Earth* trilogy by N. K. Jemisin and have just begun *Black Leopard, Red Wolf* by Marlon James. One of my favorite books is *Possession* by A. S. Byatt."

**Josh Kalscheur**: *New Dark Ages* by Donald Revell; *Snowflake / different streets* by Eileen Myles; *Steps* by Jerzy Kosinski; *Molloy by Samuel Beckett; Lost Alphabet* by Lisa Olstein; *The Performance of Becoming Human* by Daniel Bortzuzky; *Revolver* by Robyn Schiff; *Don't Let Me Be Lonely* by Claudia Rankine; *My Year of Rest and Relaxation* by Ottessa Moshfegh; *The Berlin Stories* by Robert Walser; *The Collected Poems of Robert Creeley, 1945-1975 ; Up Jump the Boogie* by John Murillo.

**Ji yoon Lee** is a poet and translator whose most recent publication is a book of translation, *Cheer Up Femme Fatale* (Action Books 2015). She is the author of *Foreigner's Folly* (Coconut Books, 2014), *Funsize/Bitesize* (Birds of Lace, 2013), and *IMMA* (Radioactive Moat, 2012). She was born in South Korea, and immigrated to the United States as a teen. This poem is part of a manuscript, tentatively titled, BABY VISA DENIED, which explores her autobiographical self-storytelling regarding her early experience of separation from her parents due to her being denied of her visa as an infant, and her immigration as a teen. The shadows (Wire mother, Cloth mother) of Harry Harlow's attachment experiment keep intruding on these poems to make this storytelling difficult.

**Rachel Levitsky**: "Dear Rebecca,
In my brain I over-responded to your contributors' reading list request. I wondered should I talk about being a reader of Caroline Bergvall's *Alyson Singes*, forthcoming title from Nightboat? What are the ethics of disclosing that. Do I ask Caroline before telling. Do I tell that Belladonna* and Emily Beall published an art book edition of 75, ten years ago, a much shorter version. *Alyson* comes out from Chaucer's Canterbury Tales (Wife of Bath) speaks Chaucerian and is a vehicle for a free feminism and also in the hands of Bergvall a lesson on how any of us can of course read Chaucer and even be liberated by it. At least by reading her take. So yes! I'm super thrilled by this big book coming next Fall. Or that I was in Paris for Dawn Lundy Martin's Poets and Critics and the release in French of *Discipline* (published in French by Joco Seria, in English by Nightboat), so rereading *Discipline*. Or now while I'm writing to you for reals loving reading Lonely Christopher's *The Resignation* (Roof) preparing for my reading with Lonely at the Project tonight and also to my right is the stunning stupendous and more exclamation new anthology edited by Erica Hunt and Dawn Lundy Martin: *Letters to the Future: Black Women/Radical Writing*, just recently out from Kore Press and to be used as a textbook in my Freshman Studio—which makes me giddy."

**Kevin McWha Steele**: Some favorites: Kundera—*The Book of Laughter and Forgetting*, Rich—*The Fact of a Doorframe*, Sartre—*The Chips Are Down*, Poe—*Metzengerstein*, Yau—*Radiant Silhouette*, De Beauvoir— *The Ethics of Ambiguity*, O'Connor—*Three by Flannery O'Connor*, Crane—*Blue Hotel*, Murakami—*The Wind-Up Bird Chronicle*, Equi—*The Cloud of Knowable Things*, Winterson—*Art Objects*, Debord—*Society of The Spectacle*, Rabelais—*The Duchess of Langeais*, Balzac—*Gargantua*, Zola—*The Human Beast*, LaFarge—*Laughing Boy*, Baldwin—*Go Tell It On The Mountain*, Nhat Hanh—*Lotus in a Sea of Fire*, Kerouac—*The Dharma Bums*, Irving—*Setting Free the Bears*, Brooks—*In The Mecca*, Fitzgerald—*The Great Gatsby*, DeLillo—*White Noise*, Baudelaire—*Artificial Paradises*, Ionesco—*The Rhinoceros*, Duras—*The Lover*, Lee—*To Kill A Mockingbird*, Silverstein—*Lafcadio*

**Claire Meuschke** is reading Mei-mei Berssenbrugge's *Four Year Old Girl*, Brandon Shimoda's *The Desert*, and articles in *The San Francisco Call* (1890-1913). Her first book of poems, *Upend*, will be out in 2020 with Noemi Press.

**Christopher Patrick Miller** is the author of *ARCH*, forthcoming from Atelos in 2019. He is currently reading Tongo Eisen-Martin's *Heaven is All Goodbyes* (City Lights, 2017).

**Abby Minor** lives in the ridges and valleys of central Pennsylvania. She is currently reading & loving Joanne Kyger's *The Japan and India Journals, 1960-1964*; Alice Notley's *In the Pines*; & Douglas Kearney's *The Black Automaton*.

**Nawal Nader-French** lives in Boulder county, Colorado with her four children and husband. In 1994, after living in Accra, Beirut, Hamburg and London, Nawal immigrated to the U.S.A from the U.K. In 2015 after a combined ten years of teaching English, developing curriculum, and coordinating eLearning for a large school district, Nawal resigned from public education to become a full-time writer. "Andrea Rexilius, Eric Baus and J.Michael Martinez are my go-to poets. At my side is always a copy of a Rexilius work and am currently rereading and taking my time with *To Be Human Is To Be A Conversation*. My reading playlist includes (on repeat), Baus's *The To Sound*, Martinez's *In the Garden of the Bridehouse* as well as Khadijah Queen's *Conduit*. I'm forever in love with Divya Victor's *Kith*, Dorothea Lasky's *Milk*, Anne Carson's *Nox*, and Renee Gladman's *Prose Architectures*. I am about to starting reading (probably simultaneously) Eleni Sikelianos' *The Book of Jon*, Nathaniel Mackey's *Discrepant Engagement: Dissonance, Cross-Culturality and Experimental Writing*, Luce Irigiray's *This Sex Which Is Not One*, Rosmarie Waldrop's *Dissonance*, Paul Celan's *The Meridian*, Ching-In Chen's *Recombinant*, and Jill Khoury's *Suites for the Modern Dancer*.

**Jesse Nathan**: *A Lover's Discourse*, Roland Barthes; *Cooling Time*, CD Wright; *Five Groups of Verse*, Charles Reznikoff; *All the Dirty Parts*, Daniel Handler; *As for Dream*, Saskia Hamilton; *Water and Dreams*, Gaston Bachelard; "His True Penelope Was Flaubert," Veronica Forrest-Thomson; *A Little Book on Form*, Robert Hass; *Maud Martha*, Gwendolyn Brooks; *Anyone*, Nate Klug; "Against Historicist Fundamentalism," Eric Haylot; *Novices: A Study of Poetic Apprenticeship*, Clayton Eshleman; *Romey's Order*, Atsuro Riley.

**Wendy C. Ortiz** is the author of *Excavation: A Memoir, Hollywood Notebook*, and the dreamoir *Bruja*. Recent favorite reads: *Invasive Species* by Marwa Helal; *King Kong Theory* by Virginie Despentes; *American Sonnets for My Past and Future Assassins* by Terrance Hayes; *Crux: A Cross-Border Memoir* by Jean Guerrero; and *Fruit of the Drunken Tree* by Ingrid Rojas Contreras.

**Ariana Reines**: "ten books I've been loving recently: *Rumi and His Friends: Excerpts from the Manaquib al-'Arifin of Aflaki* translated by Camille Adams Helminski with Susan Blaylock; *Truth of Dare: Encounters with Power, Authority, and Mystery* by Starhawk; *Sitt Marie Rose* by Etel Adnan; *The Mars Room* by Rachel Kushner; *Evolution* by Eileen Myles; *Social Practices* by Chris Kraus; *Mucus in my Pineal Gland* by Juliana Huxtable; *Ask and It Is Given* by Esther & Jerry Hicks; *Moral Grandeur and Spiritual Audacity* by Abraham Joshua Heschel; *Magdalene* by Marie Howe; *Trickster Feminism* by Anne Waldman, *Don't Call Us Dead* by Danez Smith, *Justice Piece // Transmission* by Lauren Levin, *Julian* by Julian Talamantez Brolaski, *A Song of Ice and Fire* by George RR Martin, *A Dark Dreambox of Another Kind* by Francis Starr Hamilton, *When the Sick Rule the World* by Dodie Bellamy, *Elizabeth Takes Off* by Elizabeth Taylor; and finally, my hands-down favorite of the last few whiles is *OLIO* by Tyehimba Jess"

**Clinton Siegle** grew up in Lame Deer, Montana on the No Cheyenne reservation. He is writing poems in the dark due to his eyesight and other disabilities. Currently, he is living in La Paz, Bolivia. "I just finished the story of John Colter and his trip through Yellowstone. The book was amazing. I enjoyed the insight brought out by a person who researched his story details."

**Eleni Sikelianos:** "In France, I was reading French poet Stephen Bouquet's new book of essays, *la cité des paroles*, on queerness and capital, Lorca, Pasolini, Crane, and others. Smart, fresh, and safe from the squeeze of academic thinking. Back home, I'm reading, through a form of wanton bibliomancy, various poets in *Reversible Monuments*, the 2002 anthology of contemporary Mexican poetry edited by Monica de la Torre and Michael Wiegers. Am in the midst of Anne Waldman's just-out *Trickster Feminism* (a balm, as is all poetry and art, in these off-the-rails times), and am almost done with Michael Ondaatje's new novel, *Warlight*. From Bouquet's book, in a thought about metaphor, metamorphosis, poetry, communism, capital, desire, and love: '[R]ien n'a changé depuis Ovide : la poésie produit des miracles.' ('Nothing has changed since Ovid: poetry produces miracles.')"

**Laura Sims** is the author of *Looker*, a novel, and four books of poetry, most recently *Staying Alive*. She recently read and enjoyed *A Month in the Country*, by J. L. Carr, *The Pumpkin Eater*, by Penelope Mortimer, *Lagoon and Binti*, by Nnedi Okorafor, *The End of Something*, by Kate Greenstreet, *Landscape with Sex and Violence*, by Lynn Melnick, *Mina* by Kim Sagwa, and *See What I Have Done*, by Sarah Schmidt.

**Serena Solin**: "Right now I'm reading two books by Clark Coolidge out on Pressed Wafer: *Poet* and *Life Forms Here*. Coolidge is a savant, if not an idiot. He says it best: 'What do you take me for?    a poet? / only trying to do a little good here / among the sponges in shorts and turtle prints.'"

**Brian Kim Stefans**: "Presently reading J. M. Coetzee's *Elizabeth Costello*, and listening to the audiobook of *Consider Phlebas* by Iain Banks, and also a lot of poetry by in particular Bill Knott, old fave Sylvia Plath, the late Scottish poet Tom Leonard, and Stephen Yenser with whom I worked at UCLA. This month I'm going to start on a long-germinating project of translating the poems of Mexican writer Gerardo Deniz (Mónica de la Torre published a selection of his work in 2000 which I loved). I'm still revising my translations of the verse poems of Arthur Rimbaud, a collection I'm calling *Festivals of Patience*. Also reading a lot of Korean Sijo (in the excellent versions by Kevin O'Rourke), a form I'm trying to adapt to English."

**Nat Sufrin** is reading *D'Aulaires' Book of Greek Myths* by Ingri and Edgar Parin d'Aulaire, *The Book of Questions: Volume I* by Edmond Jabès, *From Old Notebooks* by Evan Lavender-Smith, *The Age of Innocence* by Edith Wharton, and *Through Paediatrics to Psycho-Analysis: Collected Papers* by D. W. Winnicott.

**Mattilda Bernstein Sycamore**: "Right now I'm on a book tour for my new novel, *Sketchtasy*, so I'm reading and rereading my own text, and I decided that since I would be in LA for three weeks between East and West Coast events, there I would read *Ninth Street Women*, Mary Gabriel's dense 700-page book about the women of Abstract Expressionism, because I'm working on a future book about my relationship with my grandmother, a visual artist of that generation, and oh, I had no idea how immersive *Ninth Street Women* would be—how it charts the communal versus the individual, the drive to create, to remake, to re-form after the carnage of World War II, the demise of the old world with and against the emergence of the art market, and how each of these women reacted in such different ways. Who knew that Elaine de Kooning would strike me as a kindred spirit, now as I'm reading and rereading "A Desert Island" for *Fence*, an excerpt from my next book, The Freezer Door, and here I'm remembering a quote from Nathanaël's Pasolini's *Our*: 'We took care that the war, enclosed in our bodies, should remain driven there, the body, a falling point, the voice, an imagination maintained by the sole skin of thought.'

**James Tate**'s new collection, *The Government Lake*, will be released July 2, 2019 from Ecco HarperCollins.

**Nora Toomey**: "I keep coming back to Amanda Ackerman's *The Book of Feral Flora*. The intersections of poetry, time travel, electronics, and plants are where I want to be! Most recent books to rattle, hold, inspire are Natalie Eilbert's *Indictus*, sam sax's *madness* and Natalie Catasús's *Flight*. Also loving poetry podcasts! Thank you Commonplace, The Poetry Gods, and VS for blessing my ears."

**Tasia Trevino** is reading (and listening to): *The California Poem* by Eleni Sikelianos, *Travels in Hyperreality* Umberto Eco, *Four Calendar Cafe*, Cocteau Twins.

**Steffan Triplett** was raised in Joplin, Missouri. "Here are some current favorites whose intricacies impact my will for truthfulness: Ely Shipley's *Some Animal* (Nightboat, 2018); Kiese Laymon's *Heavy* (Scribner, 2018); Renee Gladman's *Calamities* (Wave Books, 2016); and S. Brook Corfman's *Luxury, Blue Lace* (Autumn House Press, 2019)."

**Jenessa VanZutphen** is reading *The Poetics of Space*, Gaston Bachelard; *The Collected Poems of Chika Sagawa*, translated by Sawako Nakayasu; *Gap Gardening*, Rosmarie Waldrop; *A Pattern Language*, Christopher Alexander, Sara Ishikawa, Murray Silverstein.

*Indolence*, **Alison Wellford**. Currently reading: *Cut Guavas*, Robert Antoni. All-time favorites: everything Jean Rhys.

FE
NC
E⋑